Janet Quin-H

Janet Quin-Harkin is better known these days as *Times* bestselling author Rhys Bowen, writer of the historical *Molly Murphy* and *Royal Spyness* mystery series. She has won the Agatha Best Novel Award and was nominated for the Edgar Best Novel. In the eighties, when this series was written, she was dubbed by one newspaper as "the Queen of Teen Romance." Janet/Rhys is a transplanted Brit who now divides her time between California and Arizona. You can visit her website at www.rhysbowen.com

JANET QUIN-HARKIN

Heartbreak Café

2

THE MAIN ATTRACTION

ellfie
BOOKS
www.ellfiebooks.com

An Ellfie Book

First published in America by Fawcett Books, New York in 1989
First published in Great Britain by Armada in 1989
Reprinted in Great Britain by Diamond books in 1994
This paperback edition published in 2021 by Ellfie Books
An Imprint of Ellingstar Media

alloyentertainment

Published by arrangement with Rights People, London

All characters and events in this publication are fictitious
and any resemblance to real persons, living or dead, is purely coincidental.

A CIP Catalogue record for this book is available from the British Library

Paperback ISBN: 978-0-9929330-7-4
Mobi eBook ISBN: 978-0-9929330-3-6
ePub eBook ISBN: 978-0-9929330-4-3

Typeset by M Rules

EM
ELLINGSTAR
MEDIA

Ellfie Books.
Ellingstar Media Ltd.
37 Warren Street, London W1T 6AD
www.Ellingstar.com

www.HeartbreakCafe.LA

THE MAIN ATTRACTION

Chapter One

One good thing about working at the Heartbreak Cafe – life was seldom boring. Not that loading dishwashers, scooping fries, filling ketchup bottles, and wiping tables rank high on my list of fun-filled occupations! It was the people at the Heartbreak – itself just a run-down hamburger hut on the northern California coast – who turned a boring job into a nonstop crazy adventure. The Heartbreak Cafe was the sort of place where anything could happen, and often did.

Among my family and friends, I have a reputation for being overly dramatic. I'm always being reminded about the time I cut my finger at Girl Scout camp and fainted at the sight of all that blood. I had to have breakfast in my tent even though the blood I lost was not more than three drops. I have also been known to have vivid fantasies about improbable things. We'd have a discussion of the space programme in school, and suddenly there I'd be, the first woman astronaut to land on Mars, basking in the admiration of my fellow citizens.

But anyone who thought I was dramatic had never met Ashley. Ashley was one of the regulars at the cafe. She wore so much eye makeup that she looked like a perpetually surprised Barbie doll, and she was always on a diet – one which usually included cookies or french fries in it somewhere. She also loved to read all the sensational newspapers at the supermarket checkouts, and she would rush into the cafe announcing that men from outer space had landed in Long Beach and she'd actually seen their ship landing, or that a rock star had driven past her and blown her a kiss from his limo.

Because of her love of drama, nobody was too surprised when Ashley flung open the cafe doors late one afternoon and stood on the threshold, tossed back her long black hair, and announced, "Everybody come quick! Somebody's just been kidnapped."

Most of the cafe regulars were sitting together at the booth in the corner, where they always sat. Howard was there, of course, looking as weird as ever in a T-shirt that said, "Science Fiction Is the Only True Reality". Art was in the corner, his hair streaked blond from surfing, his nose peeling, and still wearing his sunglasses even though it was pretty dark in the corner. He liked to look cool all the time. Terry had popped in from his auto shop and had an interesting pattern of dirt splotches on his face. His latest girlfriend, Helene, was sitting as far away from him as possible, tossing little worried glances his way every time he poked an oil-soaked sleeve in her direction. Oh, and Joe Garbarini was there, too, having just carried a tray of drinks out from the kitchen. Joe ran the place or thought he did, anyway. His grandfather owned the Heartbreak, and Joe was unofficial manager since Poppa, as everyone called him, had had a mild heart attack. More about Joe later.

Anyway, they all turned towards where Ashley was standing, framed by the doorway, her mane blowing every which way, her saucer-large eyes even wider than usual, her arms waving wildly. Nobody exactly leaped up.

"Yeah, sure, Ashley," Art said with a grin. "Kidnapped by aliens?"

"No, seriously, you guys," Ashley insisted. "I saw someone being kidnapped – down behind the fishermen's cottages. This great big black limo drew up and they shoved this guy into it."

"A limo? Behind the fishermen's cottages?" Terry asked, giving Joe a knowing dig in the ribs. "What was a limo doing there, Ashley? It's hardly limoland around here."

"I just know what I saw, and I saw a limo," Ashley said, her voice rising dangerously, "and if you hurry up and come with me, maybe we can still stop this poor guy from being hauled away."

Joe put his hand on her shoulder. "Ashley, I'm sure there's a perfectly reasonable explanation for what you saw. Maybe a limo brought some VIPs down to the beach and it parked behind the cottages until they wanted to leave. And maybe there were two drivers and one was late. You know, something like that. Or a band member got lost. There are plenty of reasons why someone could be hustled into a car. It doesn't automatically mean they were kidnapped."

"But you don't understand!" Ashley yelled, shaking herself free (which shows how wound up she was – normally she'd have been in heaven with Joe's hand on her shoulder!). "I know it was a kidnapping! I just know it! The guy looked like someone real famous and he was yelling, 'Let go of me. Help, somebody!' and fighting like crazy."

We all exchanged concerned looks.

"Come on, you guys," Ashley begged, turning back to the door. "We might just be in time! Maybe he's still struggling . . ."

"I don't really see what we can do to stop a limo," Art said, looking as if he weren't about to leave his comfortable seat in the corner. "I, for one, do not intend to lie down in front of it – *or* leap on to the trunk."

"Did you get the licence number?" Terry asked.

Ashley looked even more flustered. "It all happened so fast. All I could think of was running here for help!"

"I've never seen a kidnapping!" Howard said, hurrying towards Ashley. "I wonder if there will be a shootout – bodies everywhere! People falling from rooftops – aaaggghhhhh!"

"If you really want to help, why don't you do something sensible like call the police?" I said, speaking for the first time.

Joe looked at me. "What if she's wrong? We'll all look like total dummies," he said.

"And if she's right, someone's life could be at stake," I said.

"Let's go and look first," Joe said. "We can find out if anyone else saw the limo, then we'll call the police."

Everyone seemed to agree with that suggestion. We all

streamed out of the cafe, looking like a bad comedy team from an old movie – fighting to get through the door and down the steps, almost stepping in puddles, jostling each other, and laughing. No one seemed to be taking it very seriously, except Ashley and me. I wondered what we'd do if Ashley were right, and we came round the corner and the limo was still there. What if there really were terrorists in it and they opened fire on us or ran us down? I dropped back to the rear of the group. We cut across the muddy area between the rest of the fishermen's cottages and us, came into a narrow lane – and there was the limo!

"You see!" Ashley shrieked. "I was right! Didn't I tell you? And look – that's the guy!"

"What are they still doing here?" Terry asked. "If they kidnapped him ten minutes ago, why are they still hanging around?"

"He's fought them off, see!" Ashley insisted. "Look, they're still trying to grab him."

The back door of the car opened and hands reached out towards a gorgeous blond guy who was trapped against a wall. He started to yell, "Let go of me. I won't come with you. Help, somebody!"

"Do you think they've got guns?" Joe muttered to Terry.

"Sure they do," Terry said.

"Then we'd better get their licence number and go back and call the police like Debbie said," Joe whispered. I overheard him and, even through my fright, was amazed that he was actually giving me credit for something.

But any thought of acting like mature adults was lost

because Ashley went on running forward, waving her arms and screaming, "Don't worry! We've come to save you!"

No guns were drawn, no gangsters lunged for Ashley; nothing dramatic at all happened. Instead, the kidnapped guy looked annoyed. Two faces appeared from the limo – one confused and one grinning – and a voice across the street, on one of the front porches, shouted, "Cut!"

It was then that we first noticed the lights and the cameras and the enormous crew of technicians and actors and other assorted Hollywood types milling around a collection of trailers several yards from the kidnapping site. A man stepped off the front porch, waving his arms. "Will you kids get out of here!" he yelled. "You have just wrecked the only decent rehearsal we've managed all day!"

"A movie!" Terry groaned. "Oh, no!"

We all tried to back away gracefully, conscious of the amused looks from some of the movie people and the scowls from the others. I noticed how Joe and Terry shrank back around the corner instantly, as if they didn't want to be recognized. Ashley was the only one who didn't move. Instead of being embarrassed, she stood there with an expression of wonder on her face, as if she were seeing a vision.

"A movie!" she kept muttering. "They're shooting a movie! I can't believe it . . . wow! Troy Heller! That's Troy Heller . . . I thought I recognized him . . . I'm going to faint."

She looked as if she were about to stagger back in his direction, so I grabbed her arm. "Come on, Ashley," I whispered. "You're not going to faint. Let's get out of here before you make Troy Heller mad at you."

She allowed herself to be led like a rag doll. Once we were all safely behind the cottage wall, out of sight, everyone started talking at once, giggling and laughing in embarrassment.

"Trust you to get things mixed up, Ashley. Who else would mistake a movie kidnapping for a real one!" Art said, flicking a comb through his hair.

"I'm just glad they didn't get a good look at us when we barged on to their set," Joe agreed. "We were lucky Ashley ran out ahead of us. I'd have felt like a complete fool if I'd rushed out and tried to stop them!"

"Hey, it was a natural mistake," Howard said, defending Ashley. "We didn't see the cameras at first either, did we?"

Ashley continued to stagger along, occasionally looking back over her shoulder. Her face was glowing and her eyes were all sort of glazed over. "A movie, right here . . . oh, wow!" she kept saying. "Troy Heller. I just can't believe it . . ."

I put my arm firmly round her shoulders. "We'd better hang on to her. I've got the feeling she's about to rush back on to their set again and fling herself into Troy Heller's arms," I said to Joe, who had fallen into step beside me.

"Who's Troy Heller, anyway?" Joe demanded, looking back towards the set. "You mean that skinny blond wimp back there is a movie star? What's he got that I haven't got? I'm taller than he is, and I've got better muscles . . ."

"He's rich and famous," I said, laughing. "So far, he's a rock star, but I guess he's going to be an actor now, too. Any more questions?"

"Hey, I bet I'm a nicer person," he said, going up the steps and into the cafe ahead of me. "I bet he's like all these movie stars – a spoiled, pampered, snobby brat who wants his own way all the time."

"No wonder Ashley's got a crush on him," I yelled after him. "Sounds like your double!"

He turned and gave me a scathing look before he let the door swing shut in my face.

That's how it usually was between Joe and me. Lately, it had got even worse.

Poppa had refused to take things as easy as the doctor had ordered, and he was back in bed again. Joe had been running the place, with only me to help him. So we were stuck with each other virtually all weekend and several evenings a week, without old Mr Garbarini to referee our running battle. Joe and I had been fighting since the moment we met, racing for the same parking space outside the cafe.

We were total opposites. He prided himself on his immigrant Italian background, his macho image, and his way with women. I came from the country club set. Before the Heartbreak Cafe, my attention was devoted to winning tennis matches, running the Debating Club, maintaining straight As, and assuring the happiness of my super-achieving boyfriend.

So what was a girl like me doing at a place like the Heartbreak? Not that it was a dump or anything; it was a very basic cafe, set behind the fancy boutiques and restaurants of Rockley Beach, which was both a trendy hangout for the BMW set and a good surfing beach, too. The Heartbreak catered mostly to teenagers. Poppa didn't care if the kids sat around all evening sipping a soda or two. That was why it was so popular – because nobody put any pressure on anybody else, and most of the kids who came there already had enough pressures in their lives.

I had never intended to work at the Heartbreak, though. My life until then had been strictly sheltered, and my idea of hard work was putting up posters for the French Club bake sale. But I suddenly needed a job in a hurry: my parents had split up, and I had to help pay my way and give up the sort of life I had been used to. The more Mr Garbarini made it clear that he thought I was a useless, spoiled little girl who would have hysterics if she broke a fingernail, the more determined I was to make him give me a chance.

Working at the Heartbreak seemed as bad as potato farming in Siberia at first, and just as alien to me. But I had never voluntarily quit anything I started in my life. Then, gradually, I actually began to appreciate the cafe. At school there was always an image to live up to if you wanted to be accepted. You wore what was cool and you drove the right car and you were never seen hanging around with the unpopular kids. I guess I never noticed it before the divorce, because it all came pretty effortlessly for me – until then. At the Heartbreak Cafe, nobody cared who you were or where you came from or even how much money your folks had. If you were fun and friendly, people liked you; if you were stuck up and snobby, they didn't. It was as simple as that.

The day of the kidnapping, as it came to be known, I'd been working there as waitress, cook, and general all-round slave for two months, and I was beginning to think that I fitted in pretty well. I knew how to cook hamburgers without letting them slide off the grill and into the sink, I could balance four orders on my arms without spilling any of them down someone's neck, and I got along well with the regular customers. I was even getting along better with Joe; at least, he no longer thought of me as a helpless princess or a spoiled brat. But even then, we would never have guessed that soon we'd become allies – the only two sane people in a world gone movie-crazy!

Chapter Two

I'd almost forgotten about the kidnapping by the time I went to work the next day. Dramas with Ashley happened almost every day. But when I reached the Heartbreak around noon on Saturday, I discovered that the incident, was still fresh in almost everyone else's mind. Howard grabbed me as soon as I set foot inside the door. He was looking even wilder than usual in a bright orange and black "Love A Monster" T-shirt, and his hair was standing on end.

"Did you hear?" he yelled into my face, making me almost step back down the steps again.

"About what?" I asked nervously, looking round to make sure the cafe had not been washed out to sea overnight. "Something happened to Mr Garbarini?"

"Not Mr Garbarini! The movie!" Howard yelled, dragging me inside. Other kids were standing round the counter area and they clustered round me, too, all talking at once.

"A whole movie, they're shooting a whole movie at Rockley Beach!"

"All the location shots and Troy Heller's starring and you'll never guess what – he's playing a beach bum who gets mixed up in drug smuggling."

"They'll be shooting on the beach and they'll need local

kids for extras. How much do you think they'd pay?"

My head felt as if it were about to explode. "Wait a minute, guys," I shouted above the noise. "Let me get my uniform on, or Joe will start yelling at me."

This got through to them and they let me escape to the back of the cafe and change into my uniform. I could hear the commotion, though, the whole time I was changing. Everyone was really wound up about the movie, and there were enough rumours flying round in there for a whole issue of one of the tabloid newspapers Ashley liked to read. When I finally had to come out again, Howard was waiting for me, lurking by the door in that alarming way he had, as if he'd pounce on me.

"Isn't it just wild?" Howard asked, his eyes blinking furiously behind his glasses and his Adam's apple going up and down like crazy. "A whole movie right here! You don't suppose there is a horror element to it, do you? I wonder if I could suggest one – this might be my big chance to break into movies. How about if the drug smugglers are really the undead and they rise up from tombstones and suck blood . . .?"

"They wouldn't need drugs if they were undead," I commented. "I'm sure the story is fine without any horror elements in it."

But Howard's eyes were glinting. "Maybe not the undead, maybe not true horror, but they'll need some action, won't they? How about if a great white shark almost swallows the hero just when he's trying to thwart the drug smugglers . . . and he gets away but the shark gets the bad guy instead and you see the ocean turn red as it chomps him to pieces . . . I wonder how they do that? I bet you'd need buckets of ketchup."

"Howard!" I warned as people at the tables round him looked up. "People are eating in here. I'm sure they don't want a shark in their movie! Now will you please let me get on with my work and stop grossing everyone out!"

He went and sat at his usual place, but his face was all excited and I had a horrible feeling he was working on something in his head.

"Have you seen Ashley today?" I asked him to try and get his mind on to more normal things.

He blinked as he looked at me. "Ashley? No, I haven't. I bet she's hanging round the set trying to get Troy Heller's autograph," he said.

"I hope she doesn't do anything dumb ~~again~~," I said. ~~"You know what she's like."~~

Just as my mind was conjuring up scenes of Ashley hiding in the trunk of Troy Heller's car, sitting in the corner disguised as a potted plant, or flinging herself in front of the limo, the door opened and Ashley walked in. I heard a sort of gasp go round the cafe and Howard's eyes nearly popped out of his head. Ashley was wearing the shortest black leather miniskirt I had ever seen. Her fingernails were painted black. Her hair was teased into a huge bird's nest, and her makeup, which was normally pretty exaggerated, was now overwhelming. She had on huge fake lashes around black-outlined eyes, bright red lipstick, and bright pink blush on her cheeks. She oozed her way past the tables and sank down beside Howard.

"Hi there, sweetie," she whispered to him. Howard turned bright red and swallowed nervously.

"Ashley?" he asked, inching away from her. "Is that really you?"

"Of course, honey," Ashley said.

"Ashley, why are you dressed up like that?" I demanded.

She peered up at me through the mountain of hair and layers of eyelashes. "I'm practising for when I'm a movie star," she said. "Movie stars don't have to look like ordinary people. I figure that if I look sexy enough, maybe Troy Heller will notice me. Or maybe the director will notice me. Maybe I'll be discovered!"

"Ashley!" I burst out. "Nobody could fail to notice you looking like that, but maybe not in the way you want. I've got my jacket in the closet – do you want to put it on?"

She glared at me. "No way," she said. "I look just fine. You don't know a thing about movies. I know how movie people dress – trust me."

She sat at the table and practised pouting and making little kissing sounds with her mouth, which was really freaking Howard out. If I hadn't been so flipped out myself, it would have been funny to watch him being the freakee instead of the freaker. For once I was glad to escape to the kitchen and Joe. I looked him up and down quickly.

"I'm glad to see you're not wearing tight purple pants and a gold chain round your neck," I said.

"What are you talking about?" He looked at me suspiciously, as he always did when I said something he didn't quite understand. He hated not being at least two steps ahead of me.

"The movie. Haven't you heard them in there? They've all gone bonkers. Ashley's waiting to be discovered and Howard's working on these horrible special effects."

Joe poked his head out through the doorway, then rolled his eyes to the ceiling in disbelief. "It's not as if any of them were completely normal to start with," he said with a grin. "Now it looks like we're getting a whole cafe full of weirdos!" He paused and stared thoughtfully through the doorway. "Still, the movie might bring in some extra customers," he commented.

"I'm surprised you don't want to be discovered too," I said. "I would have thought this was your big chance to show off your sexy body to the world."

He looked at me with cool appraisal. "Why would I need to show it off to the world? I already have too many girls waiting in line for a date with me." He gave me a satisfied grin.

"See? You already sound like a movie star," I said. "I can just see you saying that on a talk show."

He continued to hold my gaze. "I'm glad you've finally admitted that you find me sexy and think I should be a movie star," he said.

I felt my cheeks getting hot. "I didn't say that at all," I said hastily. "What I meant was that I'm surprised a guy with a big ego like yours didn't want to be part of the movie."

He continued to grin at my discomfort. "If you knew me at all," he said, "you'd know how I feel about phonies. Movies are for phonies, aren't they? I don't want any part of that stuff."

"I'm amazed!" I said. "We finally agree on something! And

I have to admit that I'm impressed. Most guys who think they are good-looking would have their heads turned by a chance to be in the movies."

"Not me," he said. "But I'm surprised you aren't into being discovered. Movie star is just one step up from prom queen, isn't it? You were prom queen, weren't you?"

I flushed red. How had he known? "Y-yes. Must you always say something nasty when I say something nice?" I demanded. "Boy, you must really be insecure. You have to score points on everything."

He began to pile food on to plates. "I have to get my licks in first, before you say something against me," he said calmly. "Who was telling me yesterday that I was as spoiled as any movie star?"

I felt my face colouring. I *had* got into the habit of cutting him down, too, but only because he started the whole thing! He was the one who had made me feel uncomfortable when I first got there.

I took the tray of food from the counter and carried it through the swing doors just as Art arrived with some surfing buddies. He looked round the room and saw Ashley, still pouting and kissing at the corner table.

"What's with her?" he asked. "Is she having a fit or something, or is she trying to be a goldfish?"

"She's waiting to be discovered," I commented, and started to set the plates of food down at a table.

"She's what?" Art demanded.

"The movie," I explained. "She's hoping someone will discover her."

Art looked at his friends and started to laugh.

"Hey, you guys, don't laugh," a boy at the nearest table interrupted. "They're going to be shooting on the beach. Maybe you surfers can all be extras."

Art looked even more amused. "Yeah, how about that? The world will finally have a chance to see my great body!" He peeled back the sleeve of his T-shirt and flexed his muscles. His buddy Josh began to do the same. A few girls giggled.

"What do you mean, *your* great body? How about these for biceps?" Josh asked.

"You don't have a clue," the third boy called out. "If you want to be discovered, you have to look supercool, like those movie stars do on the beach. Like this . . ." He mussed up his hair, put on his sunglasses, and opened his shirt to the waist. "Yeah, man, it's like, happening here, man," he said in a bored tone.

The others started to laugh. They got out their sunglasses and made themselves look even more ridiculous. One of the girls had a tube of coloured zinc oxide, and they started to decorate each other's faces and bodies with it, all the while keeping up the same phony surfer jive.

"Hey, dude, like, it's rad, dude. It's tubular – check it out, fer sure!"

"Hey, dude, I'm like Mr Cool, y'know. I'm like, wow, hanging loose, totally gnarly, riding the tube, baby."

"Hey, Ashley," Art called out, "it's like, wow, how about we, like, hang loose, get wiped out together?"

Someone walked over to the jukebox and put on an old Beach Boys record. Everyone was laughing or trying to sound like a super hip surfer, except Ashley, who was still trying to look like a movie star about to be discovered. None of us noticed the man come in until I turned round and saw him there. He wasn't the sort of man you would notice anyway – kind of wishy-washy looking with sandy blond hair, big gold-framed glasses, and sort of beige clothes. He must have been standing in the doorway for quite a while just looking and listening as the noise level got higher and higher.

"Oh, I'm sorry," I said. "I didn't see you come in. It's kind of noisy this afternoon. Would you like to see a menu?"

"A menu?" he asked, looking at me as if I'd asked him to recite the Declaration of Independence. "Oh, no, no thank you. No menu. Just a cup of coffee – no, wait, what's the *in* drink around here?"

"The *in* drink?" I asked cautiously. "There really isn't one. Most kids drink sodas when it's hot, hot chocolate when it's not – oh, and floats are always popular. We do a good root beer float."

"A root beer float!" he said, his eyes lighting up. "That's great. Perfect! Bring me a root beer float."

He perched himself on a stool at the counter. When I came back, he was scribbling furiously.

"This is it!" he said excitedly. "This is just the place we need."

"For what?" I asked.

"For the movie! They asked me to find a real surfer's hang-out – a place where it's all happening. And I can see this place is really wild."

"It's not normally like this," I said hurriedly. "You see, these guys are just—"

"Aren't they great?" he asked, gazing at Art, who was now making kissy faces back at Ashley. "They are so alive, so real, so typical. Mr Russom will just go wild when I tell him I've found the place he's looking for right here in Rockley Beach. He only has to walk down the block to see real teenagers interacting with each other. He'll just go wild!" He grabbed my arm. "Don't go away, will you?" he said. "I have to bring Mr Russom back right now. Don't go away!"

"Mr Russom?" I asked suspiciously.

"Our director," he said, as if he were saying "our king". "Haven't you heard of Fred Russom?"

"Er, maybe I have," I said hesitantly. I didn't like to appear a fool, or even a small-town hick.

"He directed *Hot Water in the Bathtub!"* the man said. "Didn't you see that one?"

"I don't think so," I replied, worried that he'd think my movie-going was limited to Disney features.

"A cult classic!" he almost shouted. "And he's rapidly moving up. I know he's still low budget, but he's going to hit the big time real soon – and I'm going with him. The kids love Troy Heller, don't they? You know Troy Heller, don't you?"

"Oh sure," I said, glad that I could answer a question with yes for once. "I've seen his videos."

"Well, now he's going to be a movie star!" the man said. "He's got this great teen following from the music videos. Troy Heller's going to take us all to the big time – he'll put Rockley Beach on the map!"

"That's great," I said, because he paused as if I should say something.

He blinked excitedly, reminding me of Howard. "And this place – this little joint will be famous! I know he'll just go wild. We won't have to change a thing – terrible decor, real, wild kids . . . just what we want! We'll tell it like it really is!"

Then he skipped out, leaving his root beer float unpaid-for.

"What was that all about?" Joe asked, coming up behind me.

"He's from the movie," I said, still feeling dazed. "He thinks he's discovered a real teenage hangout, and I think he wants to shoot some scenes here."

"Here?" Joe asked. "What for?"

"Because this place is full of real, typical kids interacting with each other, or so he said," I answered, starting to laugh. Joe looked round the room.

"He thinks these are typical kids?" he asked, laughing too. "Didn't you tell him they were just fooling around?"

"I tried to," I said, "but he wouldn't listen. He's gone to get the director, I think. Should we tell them that they've got it wrong, that kids normally come in here to talk and eat french fries?"

"Are you crazy?" Joe asked. "They'll have to pay us if they use the cafe in the movie. And think of the publicity! We'll be shown to the whole world as a fun place to visit. We'll never have to worry about paying the rent again!"

smart move kid. smart move

Chapter Three

The noise did not die down all day. Every new arrival to the cafe was told excitedly about the movie and the hyper mood only kept building.

"Will it still be okay for me to go early?" I asked Joe as seven o'clock approached. "Remember I asked you if I could leave early because of Grant's awards banquet?" Grant was my super-achieving boyfriend. His senior was ending, and I had to attend an average of one banquet a week with him as he collected honours for sports, academics, leadership and a few other categories they seemed to have invented just for him.

Joe looked up from the grill. There were beads of sweat all over his forehead and he looked tired. I felt a pang of guilt and had to remind myself of the number of times he'd walked out on me when he'd had a date.

"Another awards banquet?" he asked wearily.

"Sure, I told you about it," I said. "Remember I asked a couple of days ago? The banquet starts at eight."

"Just how many awards can one guy win?" Joe asked with a weary grin. "You've been going to nonstop awards banquets for the past month."

"It's not quite as bad as that," I said. "But it is the end of his senior year, and all these things happen at the same time."

"It's the end of my senior year, too," Joe said, "but I don't notice myself popping off to nonstop awards banquets. What is it this time?"

"Scholar-athlete," I said. "There are ten nominees and they announce the winner tonight."

"Just like the Oscars! Does he have his acceptance speech ill prepared? 'I want to thank all the little people who made this moment possible, especially my loyal girlfriend, Debbie, for standing by me when I was only nine-tenths perfect . . .' Then you'll get up and say how proud you are to be the girlfriend of the only guy who can leap tall buildings in a single bound while maintaining a straight-A average and remaining a warm and wonderful human being."

"Oh, shut up," I said, flicking a wet towel at him.

He chuckled as he went back to flipping hamburgers. After a silence he said, "I bet you're just lapping all this up, right?"

"All what?"

He grinned. "You know, Ms Prom Queen and all that stuff. I bet it was worth dating an alien all year just for this!"

My face turned red even though I was willing it not to. "You make it sound as if I'm just hanging round Grant for the status of it," I said. "For your information, he is a very intelligent, warm person, and I'd appreciate it if you would stop calling him an alien."

"Sorry," Joe said, expertly tipping a hamburger on to a waiting bun and topping it with lettuce. "I meant android. I keep getting those two mixed up. Lack of education, you now."

"Don't give me that line," I said sharply. "You know as

well as I do that there is nothing wrong with your education or your brain."

"Or the rest of me?" he asked, challenging me with a smile.

I gave him my most withering look, which made him chuckle again. "Well, one thing's for sure, there can't be that much more to award," he muttered. "Unless he's up for Mr Homemaker of the Year . . . Mr Advanced Needlepoint . . . Mr Gourmet . . . You did mention he was taking creative cooking, didn't you?" he said, and went on chuckling to himself.

"You are such a chauvinist!" I turned on him. "I don't see why only girls should take home ec classes. Boys will have to take care of themselves one day, too."

"That's what wives are for," Joe said.

"What?" I asked, stunned.

"That's why God invented wives," Joe said. "So that men don't have to take care of themselves!"

"I-I don't believe what I'm hearing!" I stammered. "In case you haven't heard, the Dark Ages ended some time ago. Today some men find themselves acting as home-makers while their wives go out to work."

Joe began to laugh at this. "Not this guy," he said. "I like the old way much better. Good old traditional Italian marriages: wife stays home and takes care of man, man goes out and brings home the money. That's the way it should be."

I shook my head. "I think you'll have a hard time finding a wife if you tell her your philosophy before you get married," I said.

He grinned confidently. "Listen, girls will be lining up to marry me," he said.

"Luckily I won't be around to watch," I said. "You must have the biggest ego this side of the Rockies."

He looked at me for a moment, then went back to his work. "Some guys might tell you that they think their wives should be equal, but deep down inside, every guy wants to be boss. It's only human nature." Thats disgusting.

"It is not," I said angrily. "It's just that you were obviously raised in a barn and can't be expected to keep up with the times. Grant thinks it's just fine for women to have their careers and for men to share in the homemaking."

"I wonder," Joe said thoughtfully. "We'll see next year – if you two are still an item by then. We'll see if he wants to sit through all your awards banquets and let you get all the glory."

"Of course he will," I said. I glanced down at my watch. "Look, I've got to go. Grant will be arriving in a couple of minutes and I have to change."

"He's getting very brave, coming down here to pick you up," Joe said, and his eyes still smouldered with that amused look that I found so annoying. "Has he decided that he won't get contaminated after all?"

"It's just not his type of place," I defended.

"Of course not," Joe agreed. "Real people hang out here."

"Just because someone is a high achiever does not make him not a real person, you know," I said frostily. "Grant is very real."

"Great," Joe said shortly. "Okay. Go get changed. I know he doesn't like to be kept waiting."

I started to stalk towards the door, then, in the doorway, I couldn't resist looking back.

"You know," I said, "I don't think you believe half the stuff you say. I think you just say it because you know it bugs me!"

Joe looked up. "It works, doesn't it?" he said, and grinned to himself.

I really hope thats the case with the wife + Husband Stuff too

I hurried through to the rest room and changed out of my uniform, still angry about Joe's ability to needle me. "How dare he?" I muttered to myself as I wriggled out of the ugly puff-sleeved minidress and into my own comfortable jeans. He had the biggest nerve, suggesting I was just hanging round Grant because I liked all the attention he was getting in school. Grant was a terrific person. I was really lucky to be dating him. I bet Joe was just jealous that he hadn't won awards or been chosen prom king. I stared at myself in the mirror. Could it be that Joe was jealous not of the awards but because Grant was still dating me? I wondered. "Of course not," I said quickly. "Joe's only interest in me is as a sparring partner. Nothing more than that. We hate each other, right?"

And my serious blue eyes looked back at me coldly. I remembered that evening on a lonely beach when both of us forgot that we were enemies … I switched off the memory of our kiss with great effort, brushed my hair furiously, and went out to meet Grant.

Grant was waiting for me in the parking lot, sitting on the hood of his red Alfa Romeo, looking like a commercial for men's cologne. He got up when he saw me and smiled. I was glad he hadn't come in to get me, because he was dressed in a dark suit and striped tie, as if he were about to interview for the position of the world's youngest executive. Joe would have had a field day teasing me the next day if he'd seen Grant looking like that!

"What's going on in there?" Grant asked, slipping gracefully from his position on the hood and bending to give me a kiss on the cheek. "How can you stand all that noise?"

"Everyone's really hyper today," I said, sliding on to the red leather seat as Grant opened the door for me. "They've just found out they're going to shoot a movie at the cafe and they're going to use local kids as extras. Everyone's hoping to get picked." I looked across at him and laughed, expecting to share the joke with him. Instead he looked thoughtful.

"A movie, huh?" he asked. "It doesn't pay at all badly, being an extra. How many days' work do you think they'll get?"

"Grant!" I exclaimed. "You can't be serious! You aren't really interested in being in a movie, are you?"

He gave a coughing laugh. "Me? No, of course not.

Why would I be interested in a movie? Um, what's it about?"

"Surfers and drug smugglers," I said.

He chuckled. "I guess that excludes me," he said. "I don't exactly look the part for either, although I am a pretty good actor."

I glanced over my shoulder because I almost thought I heard Joe's laugh. *This is going too far,* I thought. *Now he's even beginning to haunt me when he's not here!*

"Grant!" I began. He reached over and squeezed my hand.

"Just kidding," he said, flashing me his wonderful smile.

I looked at him in admiration. He seemed so relaxed, so completely in control of himself and content with the world as he drove up the canyon with one hand lightly on the steering wheel, the other still holding mine. It was times like this when I asked myself how I could be lucky enough to be going out with him. How had he ever noticed me in the first place? Not that I am totally disgusting to look at or anything. I'm tall and slim, and my hair is ash brown in winter, ash blonde in summer. I have eyes that look blue when I wear blue and green when I wear green. But I'm not stunning; I'm not the sort of girl people turn round to stare at when we pass in the school halls. If they did turn round to stare at me, I'd be convinced that I'd ripped my jeans without noticing or sat in a peanut butter and jelly sandwich! I could never be superconfident like Grant, relaxed and calm just before a big awards ceremony.

"I can't get over how relaxed you are," I told him. "I'm a bundle of nerves, and I'm not even up for any award."

His eyes smiled at me again. "I'll let you into a little secret if you promise not to tell," he said. We pulled up to the stop-light at the top of the hill, and he slipped an arm round my shoulders, pulling me closer to him.

"Cross my heart and hope to die," I whispered. He kissed me lightly on the lips before the light changed and we roared off again.

"Mr Gardener called this afternoon and told me that I'd won – so that I could come with a speech prepared."

"Wow, Grant, that's wonderful. Congratulations!" I said.

"So while you're getting changed, I thought that maybe you'd help me think of what to say," he went on, staring out ahead of him at the road. "I know you're really good at writing. I want to make it sound as if it's completely spontaneous and off the top of my head. I thought I'd start off by saying how overwhelmed I am, something along those lines … something like, er, give me a good opening line, Debbie."

I couldn't believe my ears. I'd just come from a conversation about how much I detested the phoniness of movies, and here was Grant, my Grant, calmly discussing how to sound as if he didn't know about his award when he already knew everything! *He'd better go into politics,* I thought. *Or maybe he was right when he said he was a good actor!*

"Debbie?" Grant asked again. "Give me a good opening sentence. Come on, you're good at creative writing."

"How about: 'This is so completely unexpected that I don't know what to say'?" I suggested, my voice so heavily laden with double meaning that I was sure he must have noticed.

"Yeah, I like that," he said, making me wonder, just for an instant, whether Joe had been right all along and Grant was an android after all. But wouldn't he have to sound like he didn't know?

Luckily I was spared the trouble of creating any more lies by our arrival at our condo. We used to live in a big, old, beautiful house, but after the divorce Mom and I moved into a condo at an awful place called The Oaks.

"Do you think you can do one of your famous quick changes?" Grant asked. "It wouldn't do to arrive late."

"I have everything laid out on my bed," I said. "I just need to shower out the french fry smell but I won't be long."

"Terrific," he said, and paused to kiss me on the forehead. We walked up the front path together, past the identical neat, characterless junipers that grew outside each window of our condominium. I shuddered as I always did when I noticed them. They were a constant reminder of how much my life had changed recently. In the old days, a landscape company had spent hours cultivating the flowerbeds that bloomed year round in a profusion of colour in every corner of our broad lawn.

"You can entertain my mother while I shower," I said to Grant.

"How's your mother doing?" Grant asked. "Is she still surviving college?"

"Pretty well, I guess," I said. "Our schedules are so crazy that we hardly have time to talk these days. In fact, I feel a little guilty that I'm never home. I'm either working or going to another senior awards night with you. I know she's got her classes and things, but I hope she's not feeling too lonely."

"Is that you, Debbie?" a voice called from one of the back bedrooms as I let us in. My mother emerged a moment later. She looked rather unmotherlike in a long, fringed skirt and a white shirt with a black and white scarf around her throat. It was on the tip of my tongue to ask if she was going to a folk dancing class, but she spoke first.

"Hi, dear," she said, somewhat breathlessly, as if she'd been running. She looked from me to Grant. "Oh, and Grant too, that's nice," she said. "I hope you weren't expecting dinner . . ."

"No, Mom, as a matter of fact I have to rush out again, another awards banquet."

She gave a sigh of relief. "That's good," she said, "because I wanted the place to myself tonight."

"Studying for another test?" I asked with sympathy, feeling a pang of guilt that I wasn't going to be around to cook dinner while she studied.

"No, my group is meeting here," she said, looking embarrassed and defensive.

"What group?" I asked.

"I've, er, a group of friends are coming over. I've, uh, joined the College Conservation League, and we're planning a rally to save the whales."

I could hardly have been more surprised if she'd announced that she was trying out for Miss America or that she was going to become a nun.

"A rally to save the whales?" I asked. "You're against whaling?"

"And anything else that destroys the environment and the beautiful creatures in it," she said defensively.

"Is this a requirement for a class?" I asked, with a nervous little laugh.

She looked offended. "Of course not. I'm doing it because I want to. Do you realize how many wonderful creatures are being sacrificed to humanity's greed and stupidity?"

"But Mom!" I glanced at Grant again for support. He was looking the way I felt, half amused and half shocked. "You were never interested in this sort of thing. You were even in favour of oil drilling! And remember when Aunt Sue sent you live lobsters from Maine? I didn't notice you creeping back to the ocean to set them free! You condemned them to a quick death in boiling water! Then you ate them with melted butter – don't deny it – *and* you enjoyed them!"

Her face was flushed. "Lobsters aren't endangered," she said hotly. "And anyway, that was before. I've had my eyes opened to a great many things in the past months. I'm becoming an aware person – maybe fully alive for the first time." She took a deep breath. "Now, if you don't mind, I have to get the place tidied up and make a dip to go with these chips before they all arrive. I wonder if I dare put shrimp in it? They're not endangered, are they? Maybe I should stick to spinach."

"You'll have the Save the Spinach brigade hammering on the door if they find out about it," I said with a grin. "Woman Shreds Live Spinach in Food Processor! Gets Six Months!"

She spun around again. "You think this is a big joke, don't you? Well, you're the one who will be sorry if you wake up one morning and there are no more whales!"

She sounded really upset, and I realized for the first time that perhaps this did mean a lot to her. I went over and slipped my arms round her waist.

"I'm sorry," I said. "I think it's great you're doing this, and I'll even think it's wonderful when we can't swim at Rockley anymore without meeting wall to wall whales and being hit in the face by flukes and having enormous faces peering at our picnics!" I put my face into hers and did my impression of a whale staring. Finally she laughed and pushed me aside. "Oh, go to your awards banquet before they give it to someone else!" she said.

And she bustled past us, her fringed skirt swaying, her scarf dangling down her back. More than once since my parents started talking divorce I had felt that I had slipped into a sort of *Alice in Wonderland* time warp where everything was suddenly back to front and upside down. As I watched my mother, skipping round and humming some funky tune as she did so, that feeling came back more strongly than ever. The gang at the cafe was acting moviestruck; Grant was preparing a surprised acceptance speech for an award he already knew he was going to get, and my mother was acting like a hippie twenty years too late. I seriously began to wonder if I was the only sane, normal person left in the universe. No, correction, I thought, there were two of us – Joe was sane, too. And that thought was the most frightening one of the whole day.

Chapter Four

"How was your weekend?" my best friend, Pam, asked me as we met by our lockers on Monday morning. I waited a second before replying because I was feeling guilty about how little time I had for Pam these days. She was ~~slightly overweight and~~ slightly shy, so it wasn't as if she had a whirlwind social life of her own. We had always been involved in the same clubs and committees at school and had often done our homework together, but since I'd started working at the cafe, I'd had to drop out of most of my school activities and homework was squeezed in between serving hamburgers and falling exhausted into bed.

Being overweight has nothing to do with having a social life.

"Pretty crazy," I said. "Sorry I didn't call you. I didn't seem to have any spare time."

"More wild parties?" Pam asked hopefully.

"Not even close," I said, attempting to balance a pile of books on my knee. "I worked both days at the cafe because it was a crazy weekend and Joe needed extra help, and I spent Saturday evening at another thrilling awards banquet with Grant. Two hours of long speeches and another plate of dried-up chicken and broccoli!"

"More awards?" Pam asked with a giggle. "Does he have enough shelf space or are his parents building an addition?"

"This one didn't need a shelf," I said. "It was a money

award. Five hundred dollars – as if Grant needed it! You wait until I'm trying to afford college. If I win an award it will be one of those large plastic trophies with winged ladies on top and blue chrome down the front."

Pam laughed. "You'll have a fortune by then with all the hours you're working."

I had finished sorting the pile of books and I banged my locker shut. "I wish," I said. "Most of it has gone into my car so far. You have no idea how much money a car eats up. My mother has even ridden her bike to college a few times to save money. But then, my mother is becoming distinctly weird. Do you want to hear the latest?"

"Let me guess," Pam said, grinning. "She's graduated from creative aggression and is now into scream therapy?"

"Worse," I said, "now she's into saving whales."

"She's what?" Pam yelled loudly enough to make a passing group of kids turn to look at us.

"She spent all day yesterday carrying an anti-whaling banner around a Japanese fishing boat!"

"*Your* mother?" Pam asked in amazement. "Is this the same mother who once had her hair done every Friday and whose social conscience was limited to the unbearable wait for a table at the clubhouse?"

I giggled. Pam knew my mother pretty well. "The same," I said, "only I guess she's changed. It seems that everyone I know has suddenly flipped. In fact, on the way to school today I found myself wondering if one of Howard's horror movies had actually come true – maybe aliens have really taken over the bodies of my nearest and dearest."

Pam laughed and started to walk down the hall with me. "They didn't take over my body," she said. "Mind you, with my body, I suppose I'd even have a tough time attracting aliens."

"Don't talk that way," I insisted. "There's nothing wrong with your body. I think you look ~~just fine~~." beautiful

"Well," Pam insisted, "one of these days I'm going on a real diet. When I'm not so stressed out by school and homework."

"If you're stressed out by school and homework," I said, "you should try going straight from school to the cafe. It's been so crazy there! They're shooting a movie down at the beach and the word got round that they're going to be using the cafe for some interior scenes. It was totally crowded all weekend. It seems like every kid in the world wants to be in the movies. They all showed up hoping to be discovered."

"A movie at the cafe? Hey, that's neat. I'll have to find time to come down and watch," she said. A dreamy look came over her face. "Is it going to be a beach movie with lots of hunks running round in bikini bathing suits?" she asked.

"I think they're shooting some scenes on the beach," I said. "It's about a surfer who gets mixed up in drug smuggling. Troy Heller's playing the surfer. Of course, Ashley has totally flipped – she doesn't even notice Joe any more."

Pam's face became even dreamier. "I bet Joe would look great in little swim trunks," she said. "He's much more gorgeous than Troy Heller."

"That's what he thinks, too," I commented drily. I still could not quite understand how Pam, of well above average intelligence, could have been reduced to a trembling mass of jelly the moment she set eyes on Joe. Granted he was good-looking, but hardly Pam's type.

"I bet they discover him," Pam went on, her voice slightly breathless by now. "I can just see him in one of those tough teen movies, you know, as a gang leader or something. Can't you?"

"I don't want to disappoint you," I said, "but Joe is the one person besides me who hasn't completely flipped over this movie. He and I are the only two who aren't acting like weirdos, waiting to be discovered." I laughed. "Isn't it amazing that we finally agree on something?"

Pam regarded me seriously. "I don't think it's amazing at all," she said. "I think it's only a matter of time before you stop pretending that you and Joe are enemies and admit that you are as crazy about him as I am."

"I'm what?" I demanded.

She flushed a little. "Oh, come on, Debbie, admit that you're really attracted to him – because he's so different. That's why you're always so mad at him. You're fighting to deny your innermost feelings. We've just been covering that in psychology."

"Psychology is a load of baloney," I snapped. "And are you forgetting a little problem called Grant? I do have a very gorgeous boyfriend and every girl in the school envies me. Why would I even look at anyone else, especially someone like Joe, who acts rude and macho?"

Pam's cheeks were pink. "Opposites attract, maybe?" she asked. "We're studying that in physics."

Then she made her exit into the physics lab before I could yell something rude after her.

I don't think it's healthy to call your boyfriend a problem

At the end of the morning, I found Grant waiting outside my classroom for me. This in itself was unusual. Grant was the sort of important person who never hung around waiting for other people. He sat with his friends in this special place in the senior quad, and anyone who wanted him had to come to him.

"Oh, hi, Debbie, I just had to see you," he said, giving me a quick peck on the cheek. The rest of my junior English class was streaming out past me, giving me envious looks, which did great things for my ego.

"What's up?" I asked. "Did I forget an awards breakfast this morning?"

"No, I don't think so," he said seriously. "As far as I know there was no awards breakfast."

"Just teasing, Grant," I said.

"Oh," he said, then smiled to let me know he'd got the joke. "No, I had to see you because I can never get you at home. I tried all day yesterday and only managed once to get your mother, but I couldn't make any sense out of her. I asked her when you'd be home and if I could leave a message, and she asked me if I'd seen the news and wasn't it about time somebody did something about oil platforms killing the ocean."

I grinned. "Sorry about that. She's taking this stuff very seriously. Our apartment has become the headquarters for saving the world, I think. One weekend, and the place has become littered with banners saying 'Save the Whales', or 'Save the Seals', or 'Save the Salt Marshes'. I was very tempted to add a few of my own like 'Save the Hamburgers', just to stir things up a bit." I slipped my hand into his. "Anyway – so, why are you here?"

"I needed to know which nights you'd be working this week," he said. "I can never figure out your schedule."

"That's because I don't have one," I said. "I used to work three nights and one weekend day, but ever since Mr Garbarini went back into the hospital, I try to help out whenever I've got time because Joe's there alone if I'm off."

"Isn't that rather disorganized?" Grant asked. I grinned. "Very," I said. "Joe keeps talking about hiring another waitress, but he never gets round to it. It's that, or that any sane, normal waitress takes one look at the place and flees."

We walked together down the hall and out through the double doors to the senior quad. Then, even though I wasn't a senior, we just kept on walking, under the leafy shade of the pathways.

"So what about this week?" Grant asked. "Will you be working every night this week?"

"I have to work tonight," I said, "but then I planned to take a few days off. I worked all weekend, even though I wasn't supposed to. I need to catch up on several million homework assignments. Mrs Garcia is being very nice about my Spanish paper, but she won't wait forever for it."

"Do you think you'll have any spare time for me?" Grant asked, sounding like a little boy who was annoyed that his mommy wasn't around all day.

"I bet I can find you a couple of minutes," I said, laughing and squeezing his hand. "What'd you have in mind?"

He blushed bright red. "I, er, need some help with my speech," he said. "You know, as valedictorian, I have to give the graduation address. I've written on a good topic, but it's missing something. It's too dull. I was wondering if you could help me to make it . . . lighter. You have a good feeling for that sort of thing."

"Sure," I said, flattered that Grant needed my help with his graduation address.

He beamed. "Great. You want to come over to my house?"

"If you don't want to work around Mom's protesters," I said. "She mentioned that they were having another planning meeting tomorrow night, so we'd better go to your house or you'll be signed up to fling yourself between a whale and a harpoon."

"Great," he said again. "Tomorrow night, then? You could come for dinner, I'm sure."

"I won't say no to that," I said. "Either I cook for myself these days or I eat cold hamburgers at the cafe."

He ruffled my hair. "Poor Debbie," he whispered. "But don't worry. Things will get better soon, I know it. And you've always got me."

I was glad Joe wasn't standing beside me. That sort of remark would have cracked him up. *But then, he has to make a joke about everything,* I thought. *He could never say something warm and serious like that to a girl!*

"Pardon me?" I said when I realized Grant had said something and I hadn't heard. I blushed, sure he could tell that I had been thinking about Joe.

"I said why don't you come over tomorrow about five thirty," Grant said, ruffling my hair again. "I hate to see you overworked and tired like this, but I did find you a better job, remember."

"I remember," I said, recalling the make-work position his uncle had offered me, "and it was sweet of you. But if life's going to be tough, the sooner I get used to it the better."

He was still looking at me the way you'd look at a cute puppy in a movie, lost in the forest, crawling under a rock to hide from storms and panthers. For some reason I suddenly found that I wanted to giggle. The last thing in the world I wanted just then was Grant's sympathy. I didn't feel sorry for myself at all; in fact, I was doing a lot better than I ever dreamed I would. I was coping with weird parents, looking after myself, holding down a job, and even keeping up with my schoolwork, which amazed me!

Grant looked round suddenly. "I guess you ought not to be in the senior quad," he said. "I don't want to get us in trouble."

I giggled. "What could they do to you? They've already given you almost every award there is, and the prom was two weeks ago. They can hardly stop you from going to Harvard for walking in the quad with a junior, can they?"

Grant nodded seriously. "It's the principle of the thing, really. I should be setting a good example." He paused, considering. "And they could get someone else to make the graduation speech – which might not be such a bad thing, unless you can spark some life into it," he added.

"Are you really having such big problems with it?" I asked.

"Not really problems," he said quickly. "I think it just needs a little humour. It needs to appeal to the masses. That's where I need your help – I'm sure you could do that so well." He slipped his arm round my shoulder and steered me out of the senior quad. "Come on, I'll walk you back to your locker."

I went back to class not sure if a compliment had been paid to me or not!

Chapter Five

When I arrived at the cafe that evening, the movie crew was there ahead of me and the place was in chaos. Kids were milling round outside the front door, peeking in and blocking the entrance for the crew, who were staggering in with lights and cables, swearing at the kids to get out of the way. Inside the tables had been pushed closer together so that the customers almost had to sit on one another's laps. The area of floor not covered by tables was a jungle of cables, which were in the process of being taped down. The movie men were acting as if the rest of us didn't exist. Joe came out of the kitchen and tried to step over a crawling man while still balancing a tray of floats.

"Hey, watch it, kid," the man growled as root beer dripped on to him.

Joe caught sight of me, inching my way past a huge spotlight.

"What took you so long?" Joe asked.

"I'm not late," I said, glancing down at my watch.

"I know that. I've just been going crazy," he said. "They're acting like they own the place and we're just a bunch of stupid kids who get in their way."

"What are they doing here now, anyway?" I asked. "I

thought they'd want to rent the place out in the middle of the night or something to do their filming."

"Ah, I don't know," Joe grumbled. "I thought so, too, but these guys don't work that way. They said a lot of stuff about 'naturalism' and 'the realistic approach'. They said if the kids were really ordering and eating and hanging out, they wouldn't have to teach them to *act* like they were doing those things."

"You wanted them here, remember," I said sweetly.

"Only because it's good for business," he said, "and it is. We never have this many customers on a Monday. And wait until people see the cafe in the movie!"

"Hey, you, kid!" a big man with a cigar stuck in his mouth growled. "Do me a favour and keep this entrance clear for us. Tell these kids to sit down and shut up or Mr Russom will be here and nothing will be ready."

Joe gave me a glance. "If it weren't for my grandfather being sick, I'd tell that guy what he could do with his lights," he muttered to me. "But I know Poppa'd like me to get publicity for this place, so I guess I have to put up with these creeps." Joe wiped his hands on his apron as he walked over to talk to a group of kids. More of them came in and crammed together at the tables. Business was fantastic, of course – too fantastic for two people to handle.

"There's no way we can cook twenty burgers at a time, and serve drinks," Joe said when we were both back in the kitchen.

"You could tell them we're just serving fries tonight – on the house," I suggested. "And only charge them for their drinks."

"Good idea," he said, making me realize how stressed out he was. Normally he'd never admit any idea of mine was good, nor would he regard me as a fellow sufferer. I went over and put a basket of fries into the deep fryer, then gave Joe a hand with a heavy tray of drinks.

"There must be a hundred people in here tonight," I said, peeping out through the hatch. "Your grandfather will be pleased. Maybe this will cheer him up enough to get him get out of bed and back to the cafe again."

"To be run off his feet one more time?" Joe asked. "No, if he's smart he'll stay in bed until this is all over."

Joe staggered out under the weight of the tray. "You know what I think," he said, turning back to me as he reached the door. "I think I'm glad these people don't come all the time." And he actually winked!

Maybe this movie was a good thing after all, I decided. If it would help Joe and me to get along better . . .

By the time the director, Mr Russom, arrived, the place was so hot I expected the ice cream in the floats to melt before I got them to the tables. The big lights were glaring down on the tables, which were jam-packed with excited kids. Everyone was so awed by what was happening that they didn't even seem to mind when the movie crew yelled at them to shut up or get out of the way. I caught sight of Ashley and Howard, sitting together at one of the front tables. She beamed at me as I squeezed past her with drinks. Her eyes were all bright and hopeful, as if a miracle were about to take place right in front of her.

"What sort of scene do you think they are going to shoot in the cafe?" Howard asked me as I squeezed back again.

"Do you think it will be a shoot-out? If so I'll volunteer to be a body. I've always wanted to sprawl across a table and ooze ketchup."

"Don't be so gross, Howard," Ashley said. "And you'd better not get ketchup on my skirt. It's fluorescent, so in case they want the lights turned down low I'll still be noticed."

Just then a little round man with a beard and not much hair on his head came in. A hush fell over the crew, as if God had just appeared. They fell into place round him. The sandy-haired guy who had ordered the root beer float a few days earlier was right behind him, clutching a clipboard. He looked round and saw me.

"Oh, hello again," he said, giving me a creepy smile that belonged in one of Howard's horror movies. "We met before. I'm Harris Barclay, assistant director, and *this* is Mr Russom, our director."

"Hi," I said.

He nodded as if a passing ant had waved an antenna at him.

"We ready to shoot, Barclay?" he asked the sandy-haired geek.

"Ready when you are, Mr Russom," the geek answered.

"Then let's do it," Russom boomed. He looked with distaste at the excited tables of kids. "Somebody shut these kids up for me. I wanna talk," he said.

"Listen up, you guys. Everyone please be quiet for Mr Russom!" Harris Barclay pleaded, with no effect. Joe had come to join in the fun. I leaned across to him. "I bet his name's not really Harris Barclay," I whispered. "I bet it's Melvin or Cecil Small." I saw Joe's mouth twitch in a smile.

Mr Russom's face was rapidly becoming purple. "If you kids want to be in my movie, you'll all shut up now!" he shouted. Complete silence followed. Mr Russom nodded with satisfaction. "You listen good," he boomed. "It costs me money to shoot scenes over, so no foolin' around, you hear me? When I say 'action', I want just regular cafe stuff, the sort of thing you do all the time. Just pretend we aren't here – all blend together. Nobody should stand out. You're just background, understand?"

He glared at the kids and they stared back at him. "Okay! Ready, Phil? Tom?" The cameramen nodded. Harris Barclay came forward with a clapboard looking important. *"It's All Happening!* Scene thirty-four. Take one."

"Action!" Mr Russom said.

Cameras began to whirr. Kids looked at each other nervously.

"Cut!" Mr Russom yelled. "What's the matter with you all? I said action! I want to see you interacting with each other. I want warmth. I want happiness, get it? Laugh, shout, be teenagers. Have a good time, understand me? Now, let's get it right this time! This is costing me money!"

The cameras started again. Kids carried on embarrassed conversations, except for Ashley and Howard, who interacted so much that they were sent to a back table. Mr Russom stopped them again. "I want to hear real conversation – real teen stuff!" he yelled. "Tell them, Barclay!"

"Come on, gang," Harris Barclay pleaded. "You know what Mr Russom wants. Real teen stuff like I saw the other day. Real surfer talk. Let's hear about wipeouts and riding the pipeline and all that real stuff."

Kids started to giggle. Art and his buddies started into their surfer routine, but not as wildly as before. Mr Russom had Art's buddy Josh walk up to some girls and have them squeal things like "rad" and "awesome", and that seemed to satisfy him.

"Tomorrow, when we get Troy Heller in here, then things will really start cooking," he said.

Joe drew me aside. "Can you come in tomorrow?" he asked. "You heard what he said – if Troy Heller's here, the place will be crazy all evening."

"Gee, I'm sorry, Joe," I muttered, "but I already promised Grant I'd help him with his speech."

Joe looked at me desperately. "Oh, come on, Debbie," he said. "I can't handle this place alone. Can't you put him off?"

"I really can't, Joe," I said. "He has to hand in the finished speech for the government teacher to okay it, and he says it needs a lot of work. It's his valedictory speech, you know. It has to be good."

Joe scowled at me. "He can't write his own speech?" he asked. "I thought the guy was supposed to be smart."

"Of course he can write a speech," I said. "He just wanted my help to make it lighter, funnier. It's too serious."

"I think any guy who's going to Harvard ought to be able to write his own speech!" Joe continued to glare.

"Lots of presidents went to Harvard and they all employed speechwriters," I said. "Anyway, I haven't had a day off in almost a week now. You said you were planning to hire someone else."

"But just this week, Deb," Joe said. I couldn't remember

that he had called me Deb before and it made me feel really strange.

"I'm sorry, Joe, but I really do need some days off," I said. "I'm way behind with my homework assignments and finals are coming up. Maybe your grandfather could come in just for a while. Or just get one of the gang to help. Ashley will probably be delighted to be a waitress. She might get in the movie that way."

"Okay," Joe said, looking away from me. "That's fine. I'll manage somehow, I guess."

"You don't have to try and make me feel bad," I said angrily. "You didn't buy me as a slave, you know. I do have my own life."

"Is that what it is?" he said, his eyes flashing dangerously. "Seems to me it's more like Grant's life. Let's go where Grant wants, when Grant wants. I don't seem to hear much about Grant going anywhere you want to go-"

"That's because he's got a lot of things happening in his life right now," I said coldly.

Joe nodded, seeming to digest this fact. "Did you ever wonder if he was just using you?" he asked. "He only seems to show up when he wants something."

"That's a dumb thing to say," I exploded.

"So tell me, has he ever shown up here at the cafe, just to say hi or to bring you flowers?"

"Grant's not like that," I said. "He's ... well, he's not like that."

"If I were valedictorian," Joe said, "I wouldn't get anyone to write my speech. I bet he doesn't even give you credit for it either. He'll be there on graduation night bowing and smiling, and I bet he just forgets to mention that the witty parts of his speech are yours."

"We're a couple," I said. "We do things together. I guess you wouldn't understand that, since you only want girls for one thing."

"Not true." A grin flashed across his face. "But if I did only want girls for one thing," he said, "it wouldn't be to write speeches!"

I gave him my best we-are-not-amused stare. "Not all relationships are like yours, thank heaven," I said. "Some are on a more intellectual level."

"And some are more boring," he added, walking through to the kitchen again.

We didn't talk much for the rest of the evening. Mr Russom kept things going at a frantic pace, and I tried to crush the guilty feelings that kept creeping back every time I thought of Joe coping alone the next night.

It's not like I owe him anything, I argued with myself. *Grant needs me more, and he surely has first call on me right now.* A little voice in the back of my head whispered that I wasn't a ping pong ball, something to be batted back and forth between people who needed me, but a person with a life of my own to lead. But I chose not to listen to it – at least not at that moment.

In fact, I decided that I had done the right thing the instant I showed up at Grant's impressive Tudor-style house the next afternoon. He had a worried look on his face and a well-chewed pencil in his hand when he greeted me at the front door. I'd had no idea until that moment that Grant was the sort of person who chewed his pencils! When he saw me standing there, his face broke into a delighted grin that melted me like ice cream on a hot day.

"Thank heavens you're here," he said. "I was about to go under for the third time. You have no idea how hard it is to write a speech without saying things that have been said a hundred times before."

I walked ahead of him into the comfortable, tweedy family room. The late-afternoon sun lit the room from across the water hazard on the golf course below. I was glowing, too, with the good feeling of being needed and being important. Grant could not finish a difficult speech without me! When I sat there on graduation day, thousands of people would be listening to my words!

"So, what's the problem?" I asked, perching myself on the leather arm of the sofa, where he had obviously been working. He sank down on to the sofa beside me.

"It's just too bogged down in statistics, I guess. I want to include all this information, but it's a question of making it sound interesting. I'm talking about the percentage of graduates from our school who go on to college, who drop out of college, that sort of thing."

"Would you like me to take a look?" I asked, leaning across to peer at the page covered with crossed-out words and scribble.

He reached up and touched my knee. "I tell you what I'd love most," he said. "I'd love you to fix something to eat. I am starving, and I haven't dared stop since I got home from school."

What and he thinks she has?!

"Oh," I said, sliding down from the couch arm. "I thought your mom was going to fix dinner for us."

He did have the grace to blush. "This golf committee thing at the club came up at the last moment," he said. "I told her I was sure you could handle the food."

I fought back a wave of anger. "You asked me over to cook dinner for you? I thought you wanted help on your speech."

"I do," he said, looking up hastily. "I really do need help, but you can only start putting in the funny bits when I have the framework of the whole thing finished – and right now I'd kill for a burrito. There's a box in the freezer and orange juice in the fridge. A burrito would keep me going for an hour and then we'll take a real break and have dinner together, okay?"

"Okay," I said, not too graciously. I couldn't help thinking that I had turned down the chance to wait on people at the cafe – and get paid for it – and watch Troy Heller in action, too! Not that I was a Troy Heller fan, but I suppose most people are fascinated by movie stars, and it would have been interesting to watch Ashley and the others react to him. Now I was heating burritos for Grant instead.

As I came back, managing an ungracious smile as I plopped the burrito down in front of him, Grant leaned out and took my hand. "You really are very special, Debbie," he said. "You've been so patient and sweet about all of this stuff. It's been great having you around. Most girls only think about themselves all the time, but you've been so considerate. I'm really going to miss you when I'm far away in Boston in the fall. We'll have a great summer together first, won't we?"

I felt the warmth travelling from his hand to mine, then all the way up my arm. How could I stay mad when he put it like that? After all, as I had said to Joe, we were a couple, and couples were supposed to help each other when they needed it. I came towards him and wrapped my arms around his neck as I sank on to his knee.

"Not now, Debbie!" he said in an annoyed voice. "You're sitting on my speech!"

I got up again. "Would you rather I knelt at your feet, or that I sat in the kitchen waiting to heat the next burrito?" I asked angrily.

His face flushed. "I didn't mean it like that, Debbie," he said. "You know I love to have you close to me, but please don't crumple my only copy of the speech." He took my hand and steered me on to the sofa beside him. "Why don't you sit right here beside me and give me moral support?" he asked, resting a hand idly on my leg. The hand was disquieting. I glanced across at him. He was already poring over the paper again, with one hand on my knee as if I were some sort of pet animal. A strange thought struck me.

"Grant, when was the last time you kissed me?" I asked.

"Oh, come on, Debbie, I've got all this work to do."

"The last time, Grant. Can you even remember? This week? Last week?"

He put his hand behind my head, pulled me towards him, and kissed the top of my forehead. "There," he said. "Satisfied?"

"Oh, wow," I said with heavy sarcasm. "I hope I can stop my heart from thumping! Is that supposed to carry me through to the end of school or all the way until you're at Harvard?"

He looked up with the sort of confused expression he sometimes had when I teased him. "Debbie!" he said, shaking his head and smiling at the same time. "Debbie! Can't you see I'm all tense about this speech? I really need to get on with it if I'm going to finish it tonight. I thought you came over to help me."

"So did I," I said, "but it seems that all I'm good for is putting burritos in a microwave."

"Of course you're not," he said. "Your sense of humour is what's going to make this speech come alive, but I'm not that far along yet. Can't you please be patient? You could be thinking up some graduation jokes, if you like."

"Okay," I said, moving away from him, across the room to the wicker chair by the french windows. "I'll sit here like a good girl. I just wonder sometimes if you even notice I'm a person."

He came across to me and put his hands on my shoulders. "Look, Debbie," he said, "when I get all these speeches and things out of the way, then we'll have more time for each other again, right?" And he kissed me warmly on the lips, making me tingle all over. At that moment I was glad that I'd missed out on Troy Heller, even if I had been demoted from speechwriter to burrito heater.

seriously? one kiss and she forgets that hes being horrible to her?

Chapter Six

After I arrived home that evening Pam called me, her voice bursting with excitement. "I was down at the cafe! Where were you?" she shouted into the phone.

"I couldn't come. I had to help Grant with his speech," I said. "How was it?"

"Terrific. Troy Heller is gorgeous and they used one girl – I don't know her name – to walk past and say hi to him."

"Was it Ashley?" I asked.

Pam giggled. "Definitely not Ashley," she said. "The director got mad at her because she crawled under the tables trying to get close to Troy Heller. All the tables started rocking mysteriously so it looked like a seance. Poor Ashley. That wimpy Barclay guy took her hand and put her very firmly at the very back."

"Did you get in the scene?" I asked.

"I didn't dare," she said. "I was dressed – well, you know how I dress, and everyone else was so trendy and beachy looking. So I just stayed in the doorway and watched. You should have seen Joe. He was crazy trying to serve all those people, but the cafe must have done terrific business all night. The director said Joe's real service gave the movie 'verisimilitude'."

"I feel bad about not being there," I said. "Joe asked me to come in and help tonight, but I'd already promised to help Grant. He had to get his speech finished."

"Did he get it finished?" Pam asked. "How is it?"

"The first draft's pretty good," I said. "A bit heavy – lots of statistics. When he'd finished he wanted me to go through and lighten it up, but it wasn't easy to do. I could hardly say, 'Did you hear the one about the two dropouts who met at the unemployment office', could I?" I paused as Pam giggled. "You know how seriously Grant takes everything. I kept having this mad desire to put a Marx Brothers routine in the middle of it. Did they finish shooting last night?"

"In the cafe? I guess so. They're going to be doing beach shots over the weekend," Pam said excitedly. "Will you be there?"

"I'll be working at the cafe all weekend. Are you coming down?"

"I might," Pam said, "if I can find the courage and a suitable beach outfit."

"Why don't you treat yourself to a new outfit?" I asked. "Who knows – maybe you'll be discovered too!"

"Discovered to be quite wrong for the movie, you mean," she said. "But I can always come down and watch, hidden under my umbrella, right?" She giggled in an embarrassed way. "It would be a good opportunity for anatomy study, wouldn't it?"

"You mean human anatomy?" I asked, laughing.

"Specifically male," she said. "Since I'm now resigned to going through life without a boyfriend, I'll just have to become an observer. Maybe I could write witty plays in my old age!"

"You nut," I said. "You'll probably be the first one of us to get married and have about ten kids!"

"Even before you and Grant?" she teased.

"Definitely before Grant and me," I said firmly. "You know Grant. He'll have Harvard, then Harvard Law School, then working his way up the ladder at a law firm, and then becoming a judge, and finally getting on to the Supreme Court to attend to before he thinks of settling down."

"While playing quarterback for the Rams at the same time?" Pam asked.

I giggled. "And when he does marry it will probably be a female of equal importance."

"The Queen of England?"

We both laughed.

"See you at school tomorrow," I said. "I still have an English paper to write and all my creative energy went into Grant's speech."

"Get him to write the paper for you then!" Pam said.

"You know Grant, he wouldn't think that was right," I said, and put the phone down a little too hard.

Pam and I didn't mention the weekend again all week. Because of exams coming up, most of our conversations were limited to discussing what questions would show up on the physics or honours English test. So I was surprised when, on Saturday morning, Pam showed up at the Heartbreak looking so different that I hardly recognized her. She was wearing a blue sundress and had her hair back in a ponytail. What's more, she was wearing makeup, which Pam hardly ever did. I got as far as saying, "Can I help—" before I did a double take and saw who it was.

"Do you like my dress?" she asked shyly. "I bought it this morning at the mall. I'm not quite sure it's really me.

"Wow!" I exclaimed. "You look great! I didn't recognize you."

She gave an embarrassed little grin. "Do I dare wear this down to the beach?" she asked.

"Of course," I said. "Why not?"

She shrugged her shoulders. "You know me," she said.

"But it's perfect," I said. "And you absolutely have to go down to the beach. Today is the big day for guy-watching. I heard they're going to be shooting some surfing shots."

"Really?" Pam asked excitedly.

"And that means Troy Heller in a bathing suit," I went on.

"Sounds good to me," she said, beaming. "Will you be stuck here, or can you come down to the beach with me? I don't know if I've got enough courage to go alone."

"I'll be able to stop down," I said. "Joe and I decided to take turns – since most of our customers are going to be extras, we won't be overworked."

"I take it Joe hasn't changed his mind about becoming an extra too?" she asked wistfully.

"Sorry," I said, laughing. "You'll have to stick around the cafe if you want to watch Joe in action. On the beach it's strictly Troy Heller surfing. Although I guess that will be pretty funny to watch. Art tells me he doesn't know one side of a surfboard from the other. They gave him one to practise on yesterday, and he tried to ride it with the fin facing up!"

"They should get Art to be his double," Pam suggested.

"They might very well use Art and his buddies in the shots today," I said. "Have a soda or something, and I'll see if I can come down to the beach with you."

Pam slid on to a stool. "Are Ashley and the others already down there?" she asked.

"Everybody is down there," I said emphatically. "Which is why it's so empty here. I'll check with Joe in the kitchen and see if he can do without me for a while."

I poked my head round the kitchen door. "I'll be back in a little while," I said. "I'm escorting Pam down the beach. She wants to watch the filming."

"Oh, sure," he said, giving me a knowing grin. "And you have no desire to be in the beach shots and get discovered and become a famous star, right?"

"Right!" I said angrily. "I thought you knew that. I am positively the least star-struck person round here, and I don't even like crowds."

He went on grinning.

"You don't believe me, do you?" I demanded.

"Let's just say that if they chose you to sit next to Troy Heller, you'd start acting as phony as everyone else."

"I would not!"

"Anyone would, except me, I guess," Joe said, turning back to the sinkful of dishes. "It's only human nature to want to be noticed and admired. Only someone like me, someone who knows where he's coming from and where he's going, doesn't care about little things like being noticed."

I spluttered. "Oh, no – who combs his hair a million times

a day? Who wore a lilac tux to his prom because Wendy wanted him to? Who acts like Mr Macho whenever even one girl looks at him?"

"I can't help it if I have natural charm," he said, "and I have to look my best for my fans."

I started to laugh. "I'll see you later," I said. "I know you're just saying all this to annoy me, but it's not working. I guess your magnetism isn't switched on today."

Then I hurried back out to Pam. We were just heading out the door when Ashley burst in. Her face was glowing bright red to match her bright red shirt, which was flapping open to reveal the tiniest white lace-trimmed bikini under it. "They're about to start the beach shots," she panted. "I had to race back up here to check my makeup. How do I look?"

"You look good," I said, "although that bikini's a little, er, *small*. It's not an X-rated movie, is it?"

She grinned. "I have to get Troy Heller to notice me somehow. I've been hanging round all week, and he still doesn't even know I exist. I'll just die if I don't meet him soon. I'm ready to do something desperate!"

"Like what?" Pam asked with interest.

Ashley shrugged her shoulders. "I don't know – pretend to drown and have him rescue me, maybe. Or pretend that some cruddy guy is bullying me and beg Troy Heller to help. Any better ideas?"

"Well," Pam said hesitantly, "you could always—"

"Don't encourage her," I said firmly, stepping between them. "No crazy stunts, Ashley. If you just stand there looking cute in your bikini, I'm sure they'll pick you for one of the beach shots."

"You really think so?" she asked hopefully.

"You look really good," I said, "and you have a great tan."

Ashley shrugged her shoulders again. "So how come no guys ever notice me – except for the wrong kind?"

"Maybe if your bikini were a little larger," I suggested, "you wouldn't give guys the wrong idea."

"If my bikini were larger, even the wrong guys wouldn't notice me," she said with a big sigh. "I guess I'm just doomed to a lonely old age."

"Me, too," Pam said. "Maybe we can play checkers together and swap knitting patterns."

"I can't knit," Ashley wailed.

"I'll teach you," Pam commiserated.

This was rapidly becoming tragic.

"Come on, you guys," I said, grabbing them each by the arm. "Let's go down to the beach. Maybe today is our lucky day and Ashley will get discovered and meet Troy Heller and Pam will meet a serious intellectual ~~who just happens to like chocolate~~ and we can all live happily ever after."

They both giggled, but I noticed they were both looking hopeful and excited. *It's funny bow having a boyfriend seems the most important thing in the world until you've got one,* I thought as I dragged them out the door. *When you've got one, sometimes it doesn't seem that great. You feel sometimes like your life doesn 't belong to you anymore.*

Chapter Seven

At the beach, we kicked off our shoes and walked across the powdery sand. More people than on the warmest summer Sunday were milling round, all trying to get close to a section beside the water's edge where lights, cameras, sunshades, and miles of black cable had been set up. The cable was by now half-covered in sand and it looked as if the beach were being invaded by a swarm of black snakes. In the middle of it all was Mr Russom, his bald head a dramatic shade of pink from being in the sun for a couple of days. Harris Barclay was scampering round, one step behind him. I watched a worried look come over his face as Ashley broke away from us and ran over as close as she dared. Troy Heller slumped in a director's chair, looking bored, his face half-hidden behind huge sun-glasses. Our gazes went down to the edge of the ocean where several kids with surfboards were standing round in a little group, talking and laughing as if the whole movie scene did not exist. Art and his buddies were among them. Pam and I wormed our way through the crowd in time to watch Harris Barclay pick his way across the wet sand to them, hitching up his jeans so they didn't get wet.

"Okay, guys, we're ready to roll," he said excitedly. "This

is your big moment. We want some terrific surfing action out of you – real exciting stuff, right?"

The surfers looked at him as if he were a sand worm.

"Now let's see," Harris Barclay said, looking the boys over. "You – I think you match his build most closely." He tapped Art on the shoulder. "You can be the stand-in for Troy Heller."

An amused grin came over Art's face. "You want me to surf like me or like him?" he asked.

"To surf well, of course," Harris said. "I want you to look like an expert. You are an expert, are you not?"

"I'm pretty cool," Art said, catching my eye and giving me a wink.

"Let's get some great action shots, shall we?" Harris said, jumping up and down with excitement.

Art shrugged his shoulders and began to walk towards the waves with his board. He slid effortlessly on to it and began paddling out. Orders were shouted and cameramen leaped into action. It was pretty exciting to watch and made me feel caught up in this whole movie stuff for the first time.

"Tell him that's far enough," Mr Russom boomed.

Harris jumped up and down, waving his arms. "No farther," he yelled to Art. "We can't focus on you way out there."

"What?" Art yelled back.

It took quite a bit of yelling until Art understood.

"You want me to surf right in here?" he shouted back.

A wave came towards him. He caught it easily, stood, and began to ride towards the shore.

"Do some fancy stuff!" Mr Russom yelled.

"You heard Mr Russom! Hot dog or whatever it is you

do!" Harris yelled. Art came in to the shore and slid from his board.

"What's the matter?" Harris demanded. "Is something wrong? Didn't you understand Mr Russom? He wants some fancy moves on those waves. He wants it to look dangerous and exciting."

"Dangerous and exciting?" Art asked, looking at his friends with a big grin. "Out there? Today? Little old ladies in tennis shoes could surf out there. It's not worth ruining my reputation." He picked up his board and started to carry it up the beach.

"What do you mean?" Harris asked in horror.

"The waves aren't right today," Art said. "I'm not riding kiddie waves. You'd better try again tomorrow."

"Tomorrow?" Harris Barclay shrieked. "But we've got everything set up to shoot today."

"You won't get any good surfing action today," Art said. "Waves are too tame."

"What's the holdup?" Mr Russom came over and demanded.

"He says the waves are too tame today."

"Then he'd better make them look not tame," Mr Russom boomed. "I'm not setting up here again. It's now or never. Does he want the job or not?"

"Couldn't you go out there and pretend they were dangerous waves?" Harris Barclay pleaded. "It's very expensive to set all this up and not shoot anything."

"Let the star do it himself," Art said. "Even he could stand on a board today."

Troy Heller got slowly to his feet. "What do you mean,

even me?" he demanded. "I used to be a pretty smooth surfer when I had more time."

Art grinned. "I saw, the other day," he said. "You rode with the fins facing upwards."

"An oversight," Troy Heller said, "and I can't risk injuring myself. Let's find another guy if this one's chicken."

"What do you mean, chicken?" Art demanded. "You ask anyone round here. Who's out riding the big ones in the winter, huh? Who can shoot a pipeline better than anyone? I don't care if he is a movie star – he's asking to get his face flattened."

Harris Barclay stepped hastily between them. "Now guys," he said. "Are you really going to quit?" he asked Art. "You don't need the money?"

Art thought for a moment. "Nah," he said. "I'm not going to let people see me look bad on a wave. Let someone else do it."

"I'll do it!" Ashley squealed. "I know how to surf, watch me. I know I could do it!"

"You do not look like Troy Heller!" Harris Barclay snapped, his voice rising dangerously. He began to run after Art, who had now picked up his board and was walking up the beach. "You can't be serious!" he shouted. "Everybody wants to be in a movie! Nobody walks out on Mr Russom! Can't we talk about this?" But Art did not even look back.

Pam looked at me in amazement. "Who would have thought that Art wouldn't do something for money?" Pam asked. "He never seems to have any."

"As long as people like Howard are around, he doesn't need any," I said. "I guess his image is more important to him than money."

YESS! THIS!

I really like Art. He doesn't care about some famous guy he cares about his sport + respect

We were distracted from that scene by a new commotion at the water's edge. Some kids were beginning to scream. As we watched, a giant octopus began to rise from the water. Huge tentacles thrashed at the surface. Spectators began to run up the beach. A cameraman tried to drag back his camera. The octopus came towards the shore. It rose halfway, then seemed to stagger and suddenly it flipped over backwards, landing upside down in the water, revealing a pair of skinny legs sticking up towards the sky.

"Do you think that was planned?" Pam asked nervously as nobody ran in to right the octopus.

"Somebody get that maniac off my set!" Mr Russom yelled.

I began to hurry towards the water. "Speaking of Howard, I have a horrible feeling I know who those legs belong to," I said. "Nobody else could have such skinny, knobbly little knees, could they?"

"Do you think he needs help?" Pam called, running after me.

Other people had the same idea. We all waded out into the waves. Some of the surfers got there first. "Help! I'm drowning," came Howard's muffled, squeaky voice, followed by coughing. His little legs waved around furiously. If it hadn't been so dangerous, it would have been very funny. I hoped one of the cameramen had been filming. It would have made a terrific movie shot. With a lot of effort the surfers dragged the upside-down octopus to the shore and pulled Howard from it, spitting and choking.

We knelt beside him. "Are you okay?" Pam asked.

Howard blinked in the strong light. "Were they

impressed?" he asked, looking around excitedly. "Did they panic? Did they think I was real?"

"Howard," I said severely. "You might have drowned. What if it had flipped over before anybody noticed? Honestly, you do the weirdest things."

"I don't see what's so weird about making special effects," Howard said. "I have my whole future planned out!"

"You might have had your whole future cut short!" I said. "Next time you want to try anything dumb, tell us in advance, okay?"

"I think it worked pretty well," Howard said in a hurt voice. "Apart from the little accident, that is. Unfortunately, the octopus was top heavy. Oh, well, back to the drawing board."

He staggered to his feet and began to drag his octopus up the beach.

"Make sure that maniac doesn't get near my set again!" Mr Russom yelled as he left, but Howard didn't seem to hear.

I leaned over to Pam. "Movies certainly bring out strange things in people, don't they?" I asked. "They sure make the weird get weirder!"

Pam was busy people-watching. "But it's worth it to see all these gorgeous bodies assembled in one place," she said. "Let's put down our blanket right here and do some serious guy-studying."

"Right here?" I asked. "We're almost on the set."

"Yeah," she said dreamily, and then turned pink.

"Pam?" I asked suspiciously. "You weren't hoping to get included in the movie, were you?"

"Who, me?" she asked, looking even pinker. "Who'd pick me for a movie? I just want a good look at what's going on. Here, help me spread the blanket out, and then maybe you can put some suntan lotion on my back. I'm horribly pale compared to all these gorgeous tans."

I looked at my watch. "I should be getting back to the cafe," I said. "It's not fair to leave Joe there alone for too long. I told him I'd be back soon."

I expected her to try to persuade me to stay. Pam was the sort of person who needed the security of a friend in a strange situation. But she was already spreading her blanket. "Oh, okay," she said. "I'll see you later then. Pop down when you can. Oh, and bring me a hamburger, would you? Or better still, get Joe to come down with the hamburger. That would really be seventh heaven!"

"One person you won't see down here is Joe," I said. "He would definitely think it was uncool."

Harris Barclay was beginning to choose kids to act as extras. I noticed that Ashley had wormed her way to the front of the crowd and began to peel off her shirt. I noticed the blush spreading up Harris Barclay's cheeks as he saw what Ashley was wearing. Then I watched him lead her across the sand. *She's finally going to get her chance,* I thought happily. Harris Barclay placed her on a towel, then he propped a huge striped umbrella over her so that just her feet were sticking out. "Poor Ashley," I said to Pam. "At least she'll have famous feet."

Pam didn't answer. She was smoothing on suntan lotion. Then she spread herself on the blanket and tried to look sexy.

"The whole world is certainly here today," she said, looking round. "Hey, isn't that Grant over there?"

"Grant?" I asked, scanning the crowd.

"In the sunglasses, back there."

I began to make my way up the beach. "Grant!" I yelled. "Over here."

Grant was dressed in very un-Grantlike fashion in brand new, brightly coloured surfer shorts, an open shirt, and designer sunglasses. He lifted them up when I called as if he couldn't really see through them.

"Oh, Debbie, hi!" he said.

I ran over to him. "You were lucky to find me in this mob scene," I said. "How did you know? Did you go looking for me at the cafe? How's Joe doing?"

He looked confused. "I, er, wasn't . . . I mean, I didn't . . . I just thought you'd be with the crowd."

"That's so nice of you to come down to visit me," I said. "I know you hate crowded beaches, and you usually avoid this place like the plague."

Grant's eyes were straying past me as I talked. "Is this the famous movie?" he asked, still looking past me.

"That's right. The famous beach scene," I said, laughing.

"How interesting," he said. "And are they actually using real kids today?"

"Sure. That's why everybody and his brother are here."

He put the sunglasses back on. "Let's take a stroll down and see," he said.

"I can't. I've just finished my break, and I have to get back to work. I really can't leave Joe alone."

"Oh, okay," he said, fiddling with his sunglasses.

"Hey, you want to come and help me for a while? Maybe I can take a long lunch break later," I suggested.

He looked as if I'd just asked him to come to a porno show or something. "You want me to help? You mean wash dishes and things?" he asked.

"It's not that bad," I said. "We do own a dishwasher."

He shifted the glasses on his nose. "I'd just be in the way," he said. "You know me – I'm clumsy round the house. I'd probably break a million dishes and get thrown out in disgrace." He glanced down the beach again. "You go ahead, Debbie. I'll just check out what they're doing here and maybe I'll join you later."

"Okay," I said. I noticed he had begun to hurry. I got a sneaking suspicion then that cool, sophisticated Grant Buckley wanted to be in the movie as badly as all those other kids. He was just too cool and sophisticated to say so.

How could he? I thought, watching him try to look cool and unconcerned while all the time pushing past other kids to get to the front of the crowd. *I never thought Grant would turn out to be a phony.* Then I remembered about the awards speech and how he had made it up in advance. I turned away from the scene and began to walk up the beach, feeling more and more uneasy. I thought I knew Grant pretty well – and Pam, too – and I also thought they were both the sort of people who wouldn't be impressed by things like movies. After all, Grant was a school leader. He was a great athlete, a member of student government – he had succeeded in just about everything. Why would he need to prove his importance?

He couldn't wait to get away from me that day, which is not the way a guy should act round his girlfriend, is it? Not if he really cared about her, that is.

I stomped up the beach, feeling angry and let down. Even my friends didn't want to talk to me anymore. They were willing to trade me in for Mr Russom's yelling and two seconds in the background of a movie. It was just another of the many portions of my life that no longer made sense.

"That's it," I muttered to myself as I pushed past the weekend crowds coming out of the fashionable restaurants or browsing in the boutique windows. The whole world had gone crazy. It really was one of Howard's horror movies come true. Aliens had invaded the bodies of everyone on the planet, and I was the only sane person left in the universe – the only person acting like myself and not some phony! My best friend was trying to look like a sex kitten, my boyfriend was pretending to be a beach dude, and my mother was now trying to save the planet single-handedly. It would be a miracle if I managed to finish high school without psychiatric help!

I stomped on, feeling the anger expanding to the boiling point inside me. Maybe I was the one who was strange, I thought. Maybe I should want to be a big star like everyone else. I let my mind wander into a daydream in which I was back on the beach and Mr Russom was choosing people for the crowd scene. As his gaze went over the mass of teenagers, it stopped, for some reason, on me . . .

"You!" he'd bellow. "Come here. Let's take a look at you. Turn sideways. Perfect bone structure for movies . . . good colouring ... Barclay! Why didn't you tell me about her before?" Then Harris would mumble something and all the time Mr Russom would be twirling me round, inspecting me. Finally he would break into a big, beaming smile. "You know what, Barclay?" he'd boom. "I think she's the one we've been looking for, the one to star opposite Troy. Come over here, Troy." And Troy would saunter across the beach, eyeing me with interest as I stood beside him, our two blond heads together, my height just right for when he had to kiss me.

"You know what, Joe?" I'd say after the shooting was over. "He's a better kisser than you are too!" And I'd laugh as I got into my car and drove away, not even seeing Grant waiting hopefully for me beside the street. I'd drive fast, the way famous people do, not stopping until I got back to our old house, which my new, fabulous salary had managed to buy back. My mother would be there, dressed in normal mother clothes, having just fixed dinner.

"You're home, darling," she'd say. "How was your day? I'm dying to hear all about it. It must be so exciting to be such a big star. Oh, your father called. He'd like you to see the screenplay he's written just for you, and guess what – he wants to take me to dinner tomorrow night." Then she'd blush prettily and her eyes would meet mine.

My daydream was so convincing that I reached the Heartbreak Cafe half intending to tell Joe that I was going back to the beach again. The cafe had filled up while I was gone and he was working crazily at the grill, cooking several orders at once.

"Hi!" I said, stepping up to remove a bun that was about to burn around the edges.

He glanced up quickly. "Boy, am I glad to see you," he said. "I don't know where they all came from."

"You must really be stressed out," I said. "That's the first time I've ever known you to be glad to see me. Can I have something in writing?"

He grinned as he slapped two burgers on to buns, threw pickles and tomatoes on to them, and reached for the french fries. "I'm changing my mind about you," he said. "I hate to admit this, but right now you're the only other normal person in the place. You're the only one besides me who wouldn't kill to be in that movie for two seconds." He looked up. "Here, take these two, would you? Table in the corner."

I carried the orders out and came back again. "As a matter of fact," Joe said slowly, "I was beginning to wonder if I'd done the right thing, letting you go down to the beach this morning. I wasn't sure you wouldn't go movie-mad like everyone else."

"Who, me?" I asked, giving a high little laugh. "You don't have to worry about me. There's nothing in the world that would make me do crazy things just to be in a movie."

"Me neither," Joe said. "Here, that's the last of the orders for now. Then it looks like we can take a break. You want me to make you a float? I think we should celebrate finally having something in common."

"Sure," I said. "That's definitely something to celebrate."

I delivered the order and then came back to sit beside Joe at the little front table.

"I have to say, Debbie," he said slowly, "that I was wrong

about you. I thought you'd never stick it out working here, but you did. I thought that you were the sort of person who really went for an image, and now I realize you're not. I even thought that maybe you were only going with Grant because you liked all the important things that were happening to him." He paused and looked at me thoughtfully. "I guess that's not true, either. I guess maybe you do actually like him – although I can't understand why."

"Of course I really like him!" I said. "You don't think I'd keep going out with a guy I didn't like, do you? What a dumb thing to say. Still, I suppose you'd never think of choosing a girlfriend because you were intellectually compatible!"

"Because what?" Joe asked.

"You know, a meeting of the minds!" I said, looking superior.

A big grin spread across Joe's face. "No, it's not normally our minds that concern me," he said. "But, as you know, I'm a more physical kind of guy myself." He raised his eyes and looked at me over the rim of the float. Just for a second his eyes held mine.

I picked up my glass and toyed with the straw. "Don't you want to take a break and go see all the craziness on the beach?" I asked. "Already this morning Art has almost got into a fight with the star, Howard has almost drowned, and Ashley was made to sit under the umbrella because her bikini is too small. The whole beach has gone crazy – everyone and his brother are down there and—" I broke off suddenly, remembering Grant and Pam. "And you ought to go see it. I'll keep things under control here," I finished hurriedly.

"You don't want to go back down again?" he asked.

"No, I've seen all I want."

Joe picked up his glass and clinked mine with it. "Cheers," he said. He didn't need to say any more. I knew he understood. At that moment I almost wanted to hug him.

Chapter Eight

On Sunday morning, the cafe was again in a state of complete chaos. At home things were even worse, so to say the least I was not too thrilled. That day my mother's Save the Planet group was gathering for another rally. Apparently the Japanese had not stopped chasing whales just because my mother had waved a sign at them the week before. Until that moment I had really liked whales and I would have joined in any rally to save them, but to be woken at dawn on Sunday morning by a whole condoful of weird people, all polluting my air with their spray paint as they wrote huge signs, was more than I could stand. In fact, I was set to wipe out the last remaining whales in the world single-handedly, just so that my life could return to normal.

I staggered out of my bedroom, fighting my way through a mob in our kitchen just in time to watch some girl ~~in Salvation Army clothing~~ pour the last of the orange juice for herself. A large guy with a flowing beard and lots of buttons on his denim jacket wrestled me for the last doughnut and won. My mother noticed me about then.

"Oh, hi, honey," she called, pushing back her hair distractedly with one hand as she poured coffee into outstretched mugs. "Help yourself to breakfast. We have to get going."

"What am I supposed to eat?" I asked. "I notice doughnuts have joined the list of endangered species!" I said, and gave the doughnut-wrestler a meaningful look.

My mother looked round with worry. "There were plenty of doughnuts a few minutes ago."

"Not any more," I said. "And there's no juice either."

"Do you have to work today?" she yelled over the noise.

"Yes," I yelled back.

She nodded. "Then maybe you can stop at the mall and pick yourself up a Danish," she called, already drifting away. "There's a dollar in my purse."

The guy with the flowing beard who had stolen my doughnut now went and put a hand on my mother's shoulder. "Come on, Margaret, we should be getting out of here," he said, almost hinting that it was her fault that everyone was taking so long to eat her food.

She glanced up at me. "I'll see you this evening, dear," she called. "It looks like we have to go now."

"Yeah, see you," I said, turning back towards my room. It was not only exasperating to wake to a houseful of strangers on a Sunday morning, but it was doubly strange to see some college guy call my mother Margaret and to watch her turning into a person I didn't know any more. So by midmorning my nerves were already frazzled by wild-looking protesters, when I arrived at the cafe to find the movie crew milling round by the locked door.

"There's one of them," I heard someone say as soon as I stepped out of my car.

"Is something wrong?" I asked nervously. My thoughts

leaped immediately to Joe. He wasn't there yet. Something must have happened. Maybe he'd had a bike crash and they were all waiting to tell me.

"We're just waiting to get in, that's all," Harris Barclay said in a whiny voice, as if I had shown up late deliberately to spite him.

"But we don't open until noon," I said. "It's only eleven ten."

"I know you don't open until noon," Harris Barclay said, looking at me as if I were a total moron. "That's why we want to get in now – so we can shoot the dialogue scenes without hundreds of customers. We were told yesterday that the manager, or whoever he is, gets here at eleven. We've been waiting ten minutes!"

He said it so accusingly that I felt myself bristle. What had happened to naturalism and reality, I wondered. "Gee, I'm sorry," I said. "I hope nobody's died of sunstroke."

"Listen, we are paying good money to use this place for location shots," Harris said. "Now can we please get inside the building? Troy hates to be rushed through his lines."

"I'd like to help," I said, "but Joe has the only key. He should be here by now. I hope nothing's happened to him."

Mr Russom arrived just then, pushing through the crowd with Troy Heller in tow. Troy had on his apparently permanent here-I-am-worship-me smile. He was also wearing surfer shorts as new as Grant's had been and a gold chain round his neck.

"We ready to shoot yet, Barclay?" Mr Russom boomed. "What's everyone hanging round for? We don't have time to admire the view, you know."

"We can't get inside yet," Barclay said, glaring at me as if I were responsible.

"Then somebody break a window and let us in," Mr Russom said, impatiently slapping his hand against his clipboard. "I want to get this over before the place is crawling with kids." He said the word *kids* like he meant *cockroaches.*

"Joe should be here any minute," I said. "Maybe he's had bike trouble."

"He cycles here?" Mr Russom asked.

"Motorcycle," I said. "I could go call his house for you – see when he left."

Before anyone could answer me, the roar of an approaching engine could be heard all the way down the canyon. Joe came into view, riding like he was possessed. He obviously knew he was late because he took the curves at impossible angles, hardly slowing at all, and screeched into the parking lot, scattering movie people as he came to a halt in a shower of gravel. He flipped open his black spaceman helmet and stepped calmly from the bike.

"What's happening?" he asked, seeing my face among the crowd.

"They were waiting to get in," I said. "They want to shoot before any customers get here."

"Oh, sorry about that," Joe said, walking easily towards the front door. "Got held up a little. Had to drop my little sister off at a friend's."

I expected Mr Russom to do one of his dramatic explosions, but instead he started to circle Joe, studying him.

"Young man," he said, "can you do stunts with that bike?"

im not being funny but im pretty sure you have to have a stunt licence to be in movies not pay kids a couple dollars

"Like wheelies, you mean?" Joe asked, surprised.

Mr Russom clearly didn't know what wheelies were. "Jumping over ramps, that sort of thing," he said.

"Sure," Joe said. "I can do anything with this bike. Why?"

Mr Russom continued to circle. "I think he'll do," he commented to Harris Barclay. "I think he'd be just perfect – same build, and with a helmet on . . ."

"What's this?" Joe asked, looking very suspiciously at Mr Russom.

"Young man," Mr Russom said heartily, "I want you in my movie! We were going to have to hire a stuntman to replace Troy for some fancy motorcycle manoeuvres, but you'd be just perfect."

"You want me to ride my bike in the movie?" Joe asked incredulously.

"That's right. I like the way you handle that machine. I think you could do the shots we had in mind. How about it?"

Joe looked across at me. "They want me to be a stuntman!" he said with a dazed expression. I expected him to tell Mr Russom to forget about any stunts, but instead a silly grin was spreading across his face. "How about that, huh?" he went on. "Me – a stunt man. I always knew I rode that bike as well as any pro." He turned back to Mr Russom. "Sure. I'll do your stunts for you. I get paid, right?"

"Sure, sure. Regular stunt fee contract," Mr Russom said. "All right?" Joe nodded. "Now that that's settled, maybe you wouldn't mind opening up the front door for us so we can get started?"

I grabbed him as everyone began to stream into the

building. "Who was saying only yesterday that movies were for phonies and he wanted nothing to do with them?" I demanded.

I thought he looked slightly embarrassed. "There's a big difference between standing round looking cute and demonstrating my skills," he said. "They've asked me because nobody else can do their stunts. That's very different."

"Oh sure," I said coldly, "very different."

I walked behind him, swallowing back all the things I wanted to say. How could a person who claimed all movies were for phonies one day jump at the chance to be a stuntman the next day?

Come on, be fair, I reminded myself. *What would you be doing now if Mr Russom had chosen you, like in your day dream? Would you have told him to get lost if he offered you a part in the movie?* Then I stomped up the steps angrily behind them because I knew that I would not have refused either and I was now jealous that my daydream had happened to Joe instead of me.

At least he'd be able to handle it, I reasoned, trying to calm myself. He'd just ride his bike, take the money, and it would be finished. At least he knew his values. I wouldn't have to worry about him.

A few minutes later, I noticed Joe watching intently while the scenes were shot in the cafe.

"Are you going to get out the hamburger patties or not?" I asked him. "They won't have thawed by the time customers start arriving if you don't."

"Can you do it?" Joe asked absently, lounging in the doorway with his eyes on Troy Heller. "I'm kind of occupied at the moment. I want to get the feel of the character I'm supposed to play."

"You're only going to be riding a bike," I said. "I bet you have to zoom through a scene once and that's it."

"But I'm supposed to be *that* guy zooming through the scene," he said. "It's a question of getting into the character. I bet he rides a bike differently from me."

"If he rides it the way he surfs, he probably falls off," I said. "Come on, you aren't taking this seriously, are you? What about all those things you said about how phony movies are?"

He turned cool, dark eyes on me. "I didn't say I was going to act like a phony," he said. "I just want to make sure I do it well. They've got to watch the picture and say, 'Hey, who was that cool dude who rode past just then?' "

I laughed. "Knowing movies, they'll probably cut your scene altogether."

"No way," Joe said. "Harris said it was integral to the development of the plot."

I grinned. "I'm surprised you knew what that meant."

"It means essential to the action," he answered.

"I am impressed. Your vocabulary has grown by leaps and bounds since you met me," I answered coolly.

Joe's eyes challenged me. "I asked Harris what it meant," he said. "He told me."

"I guess I'd better get busy in the kitchen," I said. "One of us has to do some work today." HE DID NOT!

"Good idea," Joe quipped. "Woman's place, you know!"

"Did you ever read the detective story where a guy was killed by a blow from a frozen leg of lamb, which was later defrosted and eaten to destroy all traces of the evidence?" I asked, laughing. "Frozen burgers would work just as well."

He took his eyes away from the movie scene. "I'll be right in," he said. "I just want to watch this one take."

All afternoon Joe tried hard to give the impression that the movie was no big thing to him, that he was ten times as cool as Troy Heller, but once I came into the kitchen and found him staring into the back of the french fryer.

"What are you doing?" I asked. He spun round guiltily. "Don't tell me the new fryer is broken already?"

"Oh, no," he said, coming as near to blushing as I had ever seen him. "There's nothing wrong with the fryer. I was just looking at myself. That steel reflects real well."

"Just looking at yourself?" I stifled a grin.

"Yeah," he said defiantly. "I was just wondering which is my better side – for the camera."

"Joe!" I exclaimed. "You'll be wearing a helmet. Nobody will even know it's you."

"Then I'll do it without a helmet!"

"Are you crazy? You're going to jump off a ramp with no helmet? You'd risk your life for two seconds in a movie?"

"Hey, listen," he said defensively. "I can handle that machine better than anybody I know. If I jump off a ramp, I am not risking my life, and if it's me jumping, I darn well want everybody to see it's me." But the whole point is that it looks like the [illegible]

"Okay," I said. "I guess the number of normal people in the world is now down to one. The body snatchers finally got you too."

"What are you talking about?" he demanded.

"Nothing," I said, turning away and busying myself with my orders.

I kept telling myself that I had nothing to worry about, that Joe was just naturally vain and being in a movie would not change the sort of person he was, but inside my head a volcano was building.

I had been counting on Joe to be on my side this time. We didn't agree on many things, that was true, but at least I knew where I stood with him – until now. It was therefore a horrible shock to find that he was just as easily led as anyone else. I felt horribly let down, almost more let down than when my dad walked out, stopped being a father, and started acting like an overgrown teenager. My relationship with Joe – even with our regular fights – was predictable at least, and I had started to depend on him being and acting normal. I turned to glare at the back of his head as he worked calmly across the kitchen. I wanted to rush over there and hit him or shake him, tell him to wake up and stop acting like everyone else before it was too late. I needed just one person in my life who was not going to go crazy on me. But when I tried to find the words, it just sounded spoiled and juvenile and dumb. So I kept on working and tried not to think.

Late in the afternoon Joe cornered me in the kitchen. "Look, Debbie, can I ask you a big favour?" he said.

"What is it this time?" I asked suspiciously. "Wendy's second cousin once removed is getting married in Alaska and she's asked you to drive her?"

"Nothing to do with Wendy," he said. "I just wondered if you'd work for me tomorrow afternoon."

"But Joe," I said, "I worked all weekend. I need a day off."

"But tomorrow's Monday," he said. "You know nothing happens on Mondays. You could fall asleep in here. One soda every half an hour. And I'll make it up to you. I'll give you a complete weekend off when this movie stuff's over. My grandfather should be back by the end of the week anyway. He's doing much better now."

"So what do you need to do?"

"I, er, thought I might practise some jumps on my bike," he said. "Just to make sure I'm perfect when they need me."

"I thought you were perfect all the time," I said, my voice dripping sarcasm like syrup.

"Sweet of you to say so," he answered. "I knew that, but I wasn't sure that you did."

"Hmpfff!" I muttered, unable to come up with the right crushing remark. "Pretty soon I'm going to do you so many favours that you'll owe me your soul."

"My body's better," he said, a look of triumph in his eyes.

"I'll let you know when I'm that desperate," I tossed back.

"So, you will work tomorrow?" he asked, coming up very close behind me – almost too close.

"I guess so," I said with a sigh. "Saint Debbie the Good makes everyone else's life easier. But what about her own life?"

I was very glad that evening when eight o'clock came and I changed out of my uniform.

"Are you going out with the alien tonight?" Joe asked. His calling Grant an alien struck me as rather funny at that moment, because for once he and Grant had been acting exactly alike!

"Maybe," I said coldly.

"Is something wrong?" he asked.

"What could be wrong?" I demanded. "Everybody I know, without exception, is acting like a total idiot over a stupid movie – except my mother, who's gone crazy for other reasons – but apart from that, life is just peachy keen!"

"Boy, are you in a bad mood," Joe said. "I feel sorry for Grant."

"I wouldn't," I said, grabbing my purse and heading for the door, "because I doubt he'll even notice how I'm feeling!"

I was full of angry, tense thoughts all the way home. In fact, I'd almost convinced myself that Grant would phone and say that now that he was a movie star, he'd have to break our date. But when he appeared on the doorstep, he looked just like the old Grant again: no sunglasses or goofy surfer shorts or gold chain around his neck. He beamed when he saw me.

"Hi, gorgeous," he said, stepping forward and putting his arms round me. "Have a rough day?"

"Pretty bad," I answered, feeling the tension begin to slip away.

"You feel like going out to eat?" he asked. "Something that isn't hamburgers?"

"I'd love to," I said. "How about Mexican or Chinese?"

"Fine," he said. "Chinese then. We'll have more privacy in one of those little booths."

"Okay," I said, feeling a warm rush of happiness slide through me. "I'll just go change quickly."

I went into my room and began sorting through the clothes on the floor. In spite of my mother's constant nagging, I still didn't seem to have enough time to get my room straightened out and the pile on the floor grew and grew every week. In fact, the one good thing about the conservation group was that my mother was now so busy that she didn't even notice my room any more. I finally found one uncreased shirt and a short denim skirt. I found one sandal under my bed but couldn't find the other one, so I had to settle for tennis shoes instead.

"How was the movie?" I asked tactfully through the door, since it seemed strange that Grant had not mentioned it again.

He hesitated. "Oh, you mean the movie they were shooting yesterday?"

"That's the one." *You remember, Grant— the one you were dying to get into, the one you left me at the cafe for, the one you dressed up like a beach bum for.*

"Definitely strange," he said. "And kind of boring. I didn't stick around long. But when I got back to the cafe, you seemed to be working so hard I didn't want to interrupt."

I flicked a brush through my hair, hastily patted some blusher on to my too-pale cheeks, and emerged from my room again.

"So the movie was strange?" I asked.

He had been sitting on the sofa and got to his feet as I came into the room. "Very strange," he said. "I think it's going to be a lowlife sort of movie."

"Oh, why?"

"Well, for one thing, the kids they picked to be extras. They picked the trashiest looking people – awful, badly-dressed creeps you wouldn't want in your living room. They didn't even look at any normal, well-dressed kids. As I say, I only stuck around for a few minutes, but it looked like total insanity to me."

"I see," I said, and wisely dropped the subject. At least Grant wouldn't be worrying about which was his best side for the camera, I thought, smiling to myself as he opened the front door.

"I'm really glad you thought of Chinese tonight," he said as the car roared away from our condo with the great surge of power that always scared me.

"Why, did you have a craving for Chinese food?" I asked.

"No, but the people at the next tables can't overhear us," he said. "I want to practise my speech on you. I'm not sure I am presenting the jokes properly. I'm not as funny as you."

"That's me, a little bundle of laughs," I said.

Grant turned to look at me. "Is something wrong?" he asked.

"Wrong? No, why should it be?" I said, attempting to laugh.

"*Why should it be?* I asked myself silently, staring at the wood-panelled glove compartment. *Why should I feel upset just because it seems like everyone is only interested in me when they want something? Joe was only sweet to me because he wanted me to cover for him, and Grant only took me out tonight because he wants to practise his crummy speech, which I half wrote anyway. Even Pam used me as an excuse to get to the action at the beach, and my parents don't want me around at all! Just great!*

Wouldn't it be nice if one day, somebody would want me around because I'm me?

I tried to psych myself up for Chinese food, but suddenly my appetite seemed to have gone.

Chapter Nine

"Okay, don't stop and say hi!" Pam called after me as I hurried down one of the school halls on Monday. "Are you mad at me or something?"

I screeched to a halt and waited for her to catch up. She was back to wearing her normal clothes, the glamorous look from Saturday having completely vanished. "I'm sorry," I said. "I didn't see you. My mind was miles away."

She caught up with me, breathing heavily. "I thought you might be mad about Saturday," she said.

"Why should I be mad?"

She looked a little guilty. "Because I acted a little dumb and wanted to stay down on the beach when you had to work," she said. "I felt bad about it afterwards. I cringe when I think of myself stretching out on that blanket, looking like a total fool and telling you to bring me back a hamburger or send Joe back with one. It just wasn't like me."

I smiled at her. "It's okay. I understood – really I did. There was no reason to feel guilty because I had to work. It didn't make sense for both of us to suffer – and I don't think you looked like a fool either. I thought you looked pretty good, if you want to know the truth."

"Not good enough to get picked for the movie," she said,

pushing her hair back with an embarrassed gesture. "That assistant director was so rude. He walked along the line saying, 'no', 'yes', 'too short', and so on, and when he got to me he just said, 'too fat'. I nearly died of humiliation."

"I guess movies bring out strange hidden ambitions in most of us," I said. "Just for a couple of seconds on Saturday I had the wildest urge to go and be discovered with everyone else."

"You did?"

"Yeah. Luckily I saw sense before Joe got struck with the stardom bug, or nobody would have been left to run the cafe."

Pam's eyes opened wide with amazement and delight. "Joe's going to be in the movie?" she shrieked.

"He's going to ride his bike, do stunts."

"Oh, wow," Pam sighed. "This I've got to see. When's he doing it?"

"This week sometime, I guess. He wanted me to work for him today so that he could practise riding his bike across a set."

"Are you going to?"

"I said I would, but then I changed my mind," I said. "I've finally decided that everybody in the world thinks they only have to snap their fingers and I'll come running.

"Everybody in the world?" Pam asked suspiciously.

I flushed. "Well, every *boy* in the world."

"Which means Grant and Joe?" she asked cautiously.

I nodded.

"What does Grant want now?" she asked. "Surely there can't be any more speeches to be written this year. Or does he want to get a jump on his first awards ceremony at Harvard?"

I grinned. She sounded ridiculously like Joe. "He wanted me to listen to him give his speech and to help him with the delivery of *my* funny parts. He says he can't make them sound funny."

"And you don't want to help him?"

We had reached our lockers. I wrenched mine open, sending a cascade of books and papers to the floor. "Rats," I muttered, and began to pick the stuff up. Pam squatted to help.

"Here," she said.

"Thanks." I stood up and shoved it all back into the locker. "I did some serious thinking last night when I got home," I said. "I began to wonder if I was too eager to please other people."

"You mean boys?" she asked. "I don't notice you being too eager to please me."

"Okay, boys," I said. "Am I too nice? They seem to take it for granted that I'll drop everything whenever they call."

Pam grinned. "Maybe that's just boys' egos," she said. "You know, they still believe that women were put on this planet solely to stand one pace behind them in case they need something."

"I think you're right," I said. "That's exactly how Joe and Grant have been behaving. Joe I can understand because he's always acted like Mr Macho, but Grant – I don't know about Grant any more, Pam."

"You're not sure if you like him any more?"

"Oh, I like him," I said. "He's wonderful, I guess, and I do still pinch myself every time we walk through the halls together. It's just that—"

"That he only thinks about himself all the time?"

"Exactly," I said.

"Typical male," Pam muttered.

"I guess so," I said. "I don't know if I'm overreacting. I don't know if this is normal for boy-girl relationships. I just wish I'd been around boys more before I met Grant. I wish I knew what boys were thinking."

"I can tell you what boys are thinking," Pam said firmly. "They are all thinking sex!"

I giggled. "I wish Grant would think sex – or at least cuddling – a little more," I said wistfully. "All he thinks about is speeches."

"I'm sure Joe doesn't think speeches," Pam teased.

I sorted out my books and closed my locker again. "No, Joe does not think speeches," I agreed as we began to move down the hall. "But Joe also expects me to come running when he wants something. He was mad because I told him I needed a day off after the weekend. He doesn't think that my life or my schoolwork matter at all."

"But you're not going to work for him?"

"Or help Grant with the funny parts of his speech," I said firmly. "I've decided that it's time Debbie Lesley does what Debbie Lesley wants sometimes. After all, I am a person, too, aren't I? I'm pretty smart and I'm making my own money, and I'm going to be a senior soon, and I get along with the kids at the cafe – it's about time I made a stand for my own identity!"

"Right on, sister!" Pam said, so loudly that the group ahead of us looked back and began to giggle.

We reached my classroom. "There's only one thing, Pam," I said as I began to walk away from her.

"And that is?"

"If wanting to do my own thing and be my own person is right, how come I feel so guilty?"

"Male mind conditioning," she said. "You'll grow out of it. Just hang in there. Take your days off and don't let anyone talk you out of them."

"I won't!" I said.

"Which means you'll be free this evening," she said hopefully. "I have to make all these decorations for the French Club dinner. Any chance you'd like to help?"

I gave her my most withering look. She giggled. "Just testing," she said, and disappeared down the hall.

I had a great time the next two nights, doing homework, listening to tapes, and eating ice cream. I even made dinner one night. My mother appeared briefly just in time to eat, kiss me quickly, and tell me how much she appreciated me before hurrying out to her next planning session to save some creature or other. And during two whole evenings, I only felt guilty every hour or so.

On Wednesday, when I showed up for work at the cafe, I expected to find a sulky Joe, mad at me for taking two well-deserved days off. Instead I hardly recognized him. He was dressed in tight black leather pants and an open-necked white shirt, and had a new leather jacket flung over one shoulder. I walked in to find him standing in front of the fryer, styling his hair, slicking the sides back and pulling a cute little curl down over his forehead. As I watched, he took out a can of hairspray and sprayed his hair lavishly. The spray made me cough and he spun round, looking embarrassed.

"Oh, it's only you," he muttered. "I didn't see you come in. I was just, er, freshening up."

"What's this all about?" I asked. "Big date with Wendy?"

"Wendy?" he asked, as if he had forgotten the name of the girl who had made him act like an idiot for the past month. "No, this is for the movie. We're shooting today."

"No kidding? You get to ride your bike today?"

"That's right. I get to do two scenes. We rehearsed them yesterday and the director said he really liked the way I handled the bike."

"I hope you managed to find someone to take over here while you got your practice in," I said, guilt rearing its ugly head again.

"It's okay. I just cut school," he said with a cocky grin.

"Joe!" He grinned even more at my horrified face.

"So what can they do to me? I've only got a couple more weeks and then I'm out of there. I never learned a thing in their dumb classes anyway."

"So now you're all set for stardom, huh?"

I expected him to react to my quip – either to laugh or to put me in my place. Instead he just nodded. "Looks that way," he said, "and stuntwork sure pays more than working at a crummy cafe. In fact, if this movie goes well, I'm thinking of moving to Hollywood in the summer and becoming a professional stuntman."

"You're not!" I said, grinning because I didn't believe him.

"What's so wrong with that?" he demanded. "What else can I do that makes me more than a hundred dollars a day?"

"You're not serious, Joe!"

"I am!"

"But what abput college? You had big plans for yourself. And everyone knows that the movie industry is just about the hardest thing in the world to get work in."

"Not if you're good enough," Joe said, with a very smug smile. "And if you've got it, you've got it."

He began to pace the kitchen. "Don't bother with the grill yet," he called to me. "Nobody's going to want to eat until they've seen me do my stuff. In fact, why don't we stay closed until the shooting's over? That way you can watch me too."

"Can I really?" I asked sweetly. "You're too good to me, master."

He grinned, flicked the corner of a kitchen towel at me, and strode – actually swaggered – ahead of me out of the kitchen. I noticed that he had polished his boots, too.

"Don't talk to me for a while," he said. "I have to get my motivation right for the big scene. I have to feel the anger and the triumph when I outrun the drug gang."

He continued to walk round the cafe, experimenting with keeping his hands in his pockets, hanging the jacket over his left shoulder, hanging the jacket on the right, choosing from among his roll, slouch and swagger. I watched him out of the corner of my eye as I pretended to work, conflicting emotions struggling inside me. One moment I wanted to laugh and tease him because he looked so funny, the next I didn't dare laugh because I could see that this all meant a lot to him. Then a great wave of fury would sweep over me because he had let me down and joined all the other movie zombies.

Maybe he will be a movie star, I thought. *Maybe this is right for him and he will be whisked off to Hollywood and they'll sell the Heartbreak because old Mr Garbarini can't run it alone.* And I was surprised by the huge sense of disappointment I felt. I had only thought of the Heartbreak as a place to earn money, and Joe was only a guy to trade insults with. Right? I didn't realize that I would miss them both.

No one wanted to miss Joe's giant leap to stardom, so the cafe emptied out when Harris Barclay came to tell Joe they were ready for him. Joe, who didn't want to deprive even me of this once-in-a-lifetime opportunity, pulled a "Closed for Filming" sign from out of nowhere to hang on the door as we left.

A whole group of kids was hanging around outside. They greeted Joe as if he were Troy Heller instead of Troy's stand-in; everyone was milling round him and even trying to touch his sleeve.

"Hey, guys, don't mess up my hair!" he warned. "This is *it* – the big one. You all coming to watch me?" He did his half-roll, half-swagger over to his bike, which, I noticed, had also been polished.

"Couldn't I ride on the back of your bike, Joe? Please? Please?" Ashley begged, clinging to his arm.

Joe put his hand under her chin. "Of course you can't ride my bike with me. It's not in the script. But tell you what, Ashley, you can always start my fan club if you want to," he said, smiling at her. He drew her towards him, gave her lips a brushing kiss, and let her go again. "And you can always say you knew me way back when I was a nobody."

Ashley had gone very red and was staggering round like

a person in a dream. I grabbed her arm. "Hey, Ashley, come on. We'll go watch him together."

"Isn't he wonderful?" she breathed. "I always knew he was destined for greatness. It said so in his horoscope this week, too. He's a Taurus, you know. They are so strong, anyway."

Other girls had joined us. "You're so lucky, Ashley. He kissed you!" her friend Kelly gasped. "You should blot that with a tissue and save it for when he's famous."

"He was saying he might be asked to do more than ride the bike in the movie," more voices joined in.

"Yeah, he said they were writing in dialogue for him! Maybe even making him Troy Heller's partner."

"He's going to Hollywood next week!"

"They've already asked him to star in a movie!"

"I heard a TV series."

"And you can say he kissed you, Ashley. You've got us for witnesses."

Rumours were flying round. We were swept along in a tide of admirers to the alley where the scene was being shot. I still couldn't shake off the anger I felt that Joe, of anybody I knew, had sold out to second-rate creeps like Harris Barclay and Mr Russom. The lights and cameras were already in place, and Harris Barclay was looking nervous as always. No sign of Troy Heller. Obviously he didn't want to watch Joe ride a bike better than he could. Ashley went straight up to Harris Barclay, who flinched when he saw her coming.

"Aren't you going to have a part for me today?" she whimpered.

"Not today, Ashley," he said, trying to slip past her. "It's all bike riding. No extras."

"How about if I play a girl who almost gets run down by the bike, to make the scene seem extra dangerous?" she suggested hopefully.

"No. The insurance company wouldn't like it."

"Then how about if he saves me from the gang and drags me on to his bike with him?"

"No, Ashley. Now please get out of here before Mr Russom arrives," Harris pleaded. "You know what his temper's like."

"Come over here, Ashley," I said, leading her firmly away from the set. "We'll have a perfect view from these steps."

"Yes, all you kids get way back from the set," Harris shouted, his voice already rising dangerously high.

"Yeah, guys, I don't want to run anybody down by mistake," Joe added. "Anyone who makes me skid on my bike is going to get it." He climbed off the bike and sauntered over to Harris.

"Okay, Mr Barclay. Let's run through my scene once more, all right?" he said.

"There's nothing to run through, Joe. We did it yesterday. You come round the corner as fast as you can and screech to a halt outside this building."

"Yeah, I got that, but what about the motivation?"

Harris Barclay looked confused. "You'll be wearing a helmet. Who could see motivation?"

Joe looked cool and confident. "Haven't you ever heard of body language?" he asked. "There's bike riding and then there's *bike* riding. You're talking to an expert, you know."

Harris patted Joe nervously on the shoulder. "I'm sure

you'll do it very well, and the fewer takes we do it in, the more Mr Russom will like you."

"Don't worry," Joe said. "You get your cameras working and you'll only need to do it once. It will be perfect the first time."

"That's good," Harris said. "That's very good." He looked relieved. "Ah, that looks like Mr Russom now. All you kids please remember to stay out of the way, won't you?" He trotted over to Mr Russom like an obedient dog.

"Ready to go, kid?" Mr Russom shouted to Joe. "Just like we rehearsed, remember. Let's try to get it done in one take, okay?"

"Fine," Joe said. He revved up the bike's motor and disappeared round the corner.

"Action!" Mr Russom shouted. Cameras started to whirr. The noise of a bike rose above them. Joe came into view, screeching around the corner and drawing to a stop just inches from a brick wall. It was very spectacular. Mr Russom came down from his platform and ran across to Joe.

"You're not wearing a helmet!" he yelled. "Who told you you didn't have to wear a helmet?"

"I thought it would be more dramatic if you saw my expression," Joe said. "I was trying to convey fear and anger at the same time."

"You're supposed to be Troy Heller," Mr Russom boomed. "He happens to be blond, remember?"

"Okay!" Joe said with a shrug. "I was just trying to help you make the moment more dramatic."

"Don't," Mr Russom snapped. "All right, let's try it

again – with the helmet this time."

Reluctantly Joe slipped on his helmet and the bike disappeared again. This time as he came into view, he screeched to a halt and brought a fist up in a defiant salute.

Mr Russom positively leaped down from his perch. "What was that, for Pete's sake?"

"Oh, the action at the end?" Joe asked. "Did you like it? I wanted to show that the character was not going to be scared off and would be back for more."

"No, I didn't like it!" Mr Russom began.

"Then you think maybe he should act more scared – maybe wipe his hand across his face to show he was lucky to get away, like this? Personally, I felt the defiant gesture was more in character, but—"

"Listen, kid," Mr Russom said, "if I want a shot of someone wiping their face or raising their fist, I'll get Troy to do it and cut it in. You just go ride the bike, got it?"

"I was just trying to help!" Joe said in a hurt voice. "After all, I am a biker. I know how a biker thinks. I bet that Heller character still needs training wheels!"

"Troy's a big star and don't you forget it, sonny," Mr Russom said. "Now, do you want the job or don't you?"

"Okay," Joe said. "I'll go ride."

"And let's get it right this time!" Mr Russom screeched after him. "I've already wasted enough film to stretch from here to the Empire State Building!"

Joe disappeared around the corner. The cameras started, but seconds later Joe appeared again, helmet up and riding slowly. "I've just had a great idea about this," he said. "I think we could make this scene more dramatic if we had some extras scattering as I come into the alley. Maybe one kid slips as she tries to run from my path. I miss her by inches, of course, then leap from the bike and help her to her feet. That would show what a nice guy I am, wouldn't it?"

"No!"

"Then how about if we put an old car across the alley, and a hidden ramp behind and I come around the corner and fly over the car, which crashes into the wall and explodes. How's that for dramatic?"

"This movie already has all the drama it needs," Mr Russom said, "and I already have all the headaches I need. You are just one too many. Barclay, get on the phone and get me that other stuntman we were going to use and tell him to bring a big bike—"

"Hey, wait a minute," Joe interrupted. "What's wrong with my bike?"

Mr Russom looked at him. "Oh, nothing. Nothing's wrong with your bike at all. It's the rider I'm having trouble with. And when I have trouble with something, I get rid of it. You're out, kid. Ride your bike and your motivation and your dramas out of here and let me get down to some real work!"

"You mean you don't want me in your movie?" Joe asked.

"You catch on real quick," Mr Russom said. He began to walk away.

Joe revved up his bike to a high roar. "I wouldn't want to be part of your second-rate movie," he shouted over the bike's motor. "I wouldn't be in it if you paid me! I wouldn't want to stand in for a wimp like Troy Heller. You wouldn't recognize real talent if it was handed to you with a label round its neck!"

Then he gunned the engine and roared off round the corner, leaving all of us silent and stunned in the alleyway.

Chapter Ten

One by one the kids began to drift away, all of them too stunned to say anything. I slipped through the alley ahead of them and just kept on walking. It served him right, I said firmly to myself. He deserved everything he got, trying to act like a big shot movie star! Now maybe he'll realize that I was right after all – that everything to do with movies is phony and people's feelings don't matter one bit!

Suddenly I realized I had been waiting two months for this moment! Amazingly, something had actually happened where I was right and he was wrong. I remembered all those times he had made me look inept when I was first working at the Heartbreak, like the time he found a hamburger I had mistakenly flipped on to the window ledge and the time he caught me tipping a bucketful of squid back into the ocean after I had decided I couldn't bear to cook it. On all those occasions I had sworn to get even. I had kept myself going by playing scenes in my head in which I was a top executive and Joe was my new mailboy or I was the queen of the land and he was a prisoner begging for mercy, scenes in which he was the fool instead of me. And now it had actually happened – Joe had looked ridiculous in front of everybody and when he came back to the Heartbreak I could say, "I told you so!".

The only trouble was now that I had the power to put him down in front of everyone, I didn't want to any more. I kept rerunning the image in my mind of Joe's face that second before he jumped on his bike and rode away. I had never seen Joe look like that before. Then, as I went through that scene again, I found that what I wanted to do most was put my arms round him and comfort him with a big hug – something that surprised even me!

But he wouldn't want that either, I reasoned as I turned back towards the cafe. Joe prided himself on his cool image. He'd probably show up as if nothing had happened and the movie didn't even exist! And at least he wouldn't have any more crazy ideas about running off to Hollywood and becoming a star! I felt strangely happy that nothing would be changing at the Heartbreak after all.

It was a very subdued group that met back at the Heartbreak. Joe didn't show up at all, so I began heating the grill and doing all the things he would normally do.

When I came out of the kitchen to take orders, the kids at the corner booth looked like the survivors of a battle or members of a losing political campaign. They were draped round the table with tragic faces, comforting each other and sighing dramatically.

"Isn't it just terrible about Joe?" was how Howard greeted me. "I bet you're real upset, too. If you need comforting, I hope you know that I am available." He managed to sort of leer through his grief.

"Thanks, Howard, I'll remember that," I said, moving safely out of reach.

"Poor Joe, I can't believe it," Kelly was saying over and over. "Those dumb movie people don't know a thing! He was only trying to help!"

"I can't believe he'd be so dumb," Ashley said suddenly. We were so surprised that everyone stopped talking to look at her. Usually people just went on talking over her or giggled at what she said. But this was such an un-Ashleylike remark that there was total silence. Ashley had adored Joe for longer than anyone could remember, and usually he could do no wrong in her eyes.

"What do you mean, dumb?" Kelly asked.

"To give up his chance for stardom!" Ashley said, almost choking back tears. "He could have been a big star. I know they would have discovered him and he'd have gone to Hollywood and everything. Now it's all ruined." She sank her head into her hands. "Now we'll never be in the movies. I never got my big chance and Howard nearly drowned and the waves weren't right for Art and now they've thrown out poor Joe! It's just not fair!" She brought out a box of tissues from her oversize purse and began to dab her eyes before her mascara could run.

"Come on, you guys," I said, shifting uneasily from one foot to the other. "You're all acting like it's the end of the world. It's no big thing really. I'm sure Joe's not too broken up about it. He'll probably burst through the door in a minute saying that the director was a stupid fool and that he didn't want to make Troy Heller look good anyway."

"Maybe," someone muttered, but nobody sounded convinced.

"I'm not crying just because of Joe," Ashley said in a

choked voice. "I'm crying for all of us who didn't get to be in the movie. I wanted it so bad! I tried every way I could. I'd have done anything to make them notice me! Absolutely anything!"

"You did all you could, Ashley," Art said with a wink at Terry, "and more. Maybe that was your problem. Maybe you tried too hard."

"If only they'd given me a chance, if only they'd just let me show them I'm a terrific actress." She sighed. "At least Joe got his chance."

"Why doesn't everyone have something to drink – a soda or something. Then you'll all feel better," I said, sensing that the group was about to break into communal mourning, wailing and gnashing of teeth, which would have been very bad for the cafe's image.

"I don't think I could swallow a thing," Ashley stammered. "My throat would just close up and choke me."

"I'll have a root beer float," Howard said.

Ashley's eyes opened wide again. "Maybe I could just swallow a root beer float," she whispered.

"Okay, Ashley, I'll get you a root beer float."

"With whipped cream on top," Ashley called after me, "and a double scoop of ice cream."

I grinned to myself as soon as my back was turned. Those guys, I thought. Why did they always have to make everything so dramatic? It was no big deal not to get a tiny part in a movie. And Joe wasn't even hyped up about the movie to start with. He was probably already kicking himself for wanting to be in the movie at all.

I busied myself with the orders, half listening all the time for the sound of his bike pulling up outside. But he didn't come all evening. I rushed round, working for both of us, partly mad at him that he was making me do his share of the work, and partly worried that he had had a bike accident or something. I cleaned up and closed up the cafe, then drove home, looking all the way up the canyon for signs of a bike crash.

My mother, miraculously, was home for once, sitting at the kitchen counter working on a paper.

"Hi, darling," she said. "Have a good day?"

"Eventful and tiring," I said. "You sound cheerful."

"I am," she said. "I got a good grade on my midterm humanities exam. The teacher wrote that I had insight."

"Terrific," I said. "Is that a paper you're working on now?"

"Not exactly," she said, looking up with her pencil poised. "It's a PR release. The conservation group has made me publicity chairman because I've dealt with the media before. We're going to halt a logging operation this weekend."

Although I didn't mean to, I giggled. "This is rapidly turning into the Endangered Species of the Month club," I said. "Last week whales, this week trees . . . next week you might even want to save people!"

"Very funny," Mom said, not smiling. "I don't think people would survive very long if there were no trees. We've got to stop these greedy loggers from denuding the watersheds."

I nodded seriously. "You tell 'em, Mom," I said. "I'm sure the group will volunteer you to lay yourself down in the path of the bulldozers."

She snorted. "Now don't go making any wisecracks like that when they come round for our meeting tomorrow, will you?"

"They're coming here for another meeting?" I asked with a sigh. "Mom, they're always here and there's never a thing left to eat in the house when they go. They certainly aren't trying to preserve endangered potato chips!"

"They need a place to meet!" my mother said defensively. "Most of them share apartments or live in dorms, so it's hardly convenient."

"You share an apartment," I said, "but I guess I don't count."

"Of course you count," she said quickly, "but I don't make a fuss when your friends stop by, do I? Did you ever think that I might want to have a group of friends over occasionally?"

That made me think. I realized that I could hardly remember my mother having friends. Occasionally she had PTA or ladies' auxiliary meetings, but that was all. She was not the kind of person who made friends easily. I suppose in a way, I took after her. I got along with people pretty well and had developed a few close friends over the years, but I often found myself as I did at the cafe: on the outside of a group looking in, an observer rather than a participant.

"It's okay, I have to work tomorrow anyhow," I said. "I've already taken my two days off this week. And if work is anything like today, I'll be too tired to notice if you have people here or not. Just don't let them finish the orange juice this time, please!" I gathered my stuff and started to walk back to my room. "I just hope Joe shows up tomorrow," I muttered.

"Oh – Joe," my mother said. "I'm sorry, I almost forgot. Someone named Joe called for you about half an hour ago. He wanted you to call him back."

"He did?" I asked, running over to the phone.

"Is this the rude young man with all the hair I met that night at the cafe?" she called, but I was already dialling. If Joe actually asked me to call him back, it must be pretty important.

A woman's voice answered the phone. "Hello?" She sounded suspicious and spoke with a strong accent. When I asked for Joe the suspicion softened. "Ah, yes, I get him for you," she said, implying by her tone that she knew who I was.

He sounded breathless when he came on the line. "Hi, Debbie?"

"Hi. Did your mom think I was Wendy? She seemed to know who it was."

"She knows about you," he said. There was a slight pause.

"So what's up?" I asked. "You had me worried tonight. I thought something must have happened to you."

"Er, sorry about that. I didn't mean to stick you with extra work . . ."

"But you loved every minute of it," I quipped.

Another pause.

"So, how did it go?"

"Oh, fine. Nobody was very hungry. They were all too depressed. Honestly, Joe, they were crying and acting so weird. Ashley could hardly bring herself to finish her float. You would have laughed!"

Another pause. This time I could almost feel the

uneasiness.

"So, er, they all felt bad for me?" he asked.

"Your fan club is devastated," I said. "You'll have to reassure them all tomorrow."

"Debbie?"

"Yes?"

"I'm not coming in tomorrow. That's what I wanted to talk to you about."

"You're not? Why not?"

"I, er, can't face it yet."

"Face what?"

"The kids at the cafe!" he said fiercely.

"The kids at the cafe?" I guess my voice sounded amused. "Why on earth not? They were all on your side, you know."

"That has nothing to do with it," he said. "I'd expect them to be on my side. That just makes it worse – them all looking up to me and then seeing me be a failure like this."

"A failure? Come on, Joe. So you didn't get to ride your motorcycle once across a movie set. That does not make a person a failure!"

"I got kicked out, Debbie!" he said, his voice full of emotion. "They kicked me out. That sounds like failure to me."

"But it wasn't even important, Joe. One crummy movie scene is hardly important."

"It doesn't matter what it was, does it?" he demanded. "The fact is, those kids all saw me make a fool of myself."

"Well, you did come on a little strong," I said hesitantly. "You did start acting like a hotshot a little, but that was understandable. You were flattered. We all act a little crazy when we're flattered."

"I didn't think I acted crazy," he countered. "I was just trying to make the most of the part and I failed. That's what I can't handle, don't you see?"

"Oh, come on, Joe." I almost laughed again. "Everyone fails from time to time."

"No, seriously. I could always do anything I wanted to, anything I really set my mind to, I mean. I just can't handle this feeling. I don't ever want to leave this room again."

"Joe, you're making too much of this," I said, trying to sound calm and reasonable, although part of me wanted to scream that he was acting like an idiot and making a big fuss about nothing. "Pretty soon you'll be able to laugh about it, I bet."

"Not me," he said.

"Sure you will," I encouraged. "Those kids down at the cafe all look up to you. They think you're pretty cool. They'll all expect to see you down there acting as if nothing had happened, as if a little movie didn't faze you one bit."

"I wish I could handle it like you say, Deb," he said, "but I can't. I just can't face them yet. Could you just cover for me for one more day? I have to get myself together before I let them see me."

"Okay, I'll cover for you, but I expect to see you there on Friday. I am not doing Friday night alone! So you'd better get your act together by then or you'll have to handle an angry me – and, as you know, that is far worse than any Mr Russom."

There was a pause again. I imagined him smiling. "Okay,

Aww ♡

slave driver," he said. "I'll be there Friday."

There was another, longer pause. I began to wonder if he'd gone away. Then he said, "Deb, thanks for talking to me. And thanks for not putting me down. I know we haven't always got along too well and I know this would have been a great opportunity for you to get even. I won't forget this. I owe you one." I love this side of their relationship

"No sweat," I said. "You took the trouble to listen to my problems once, and I appreciated that."

"That was no trouble at all," he said, reminding me that the scene had ended far more romantically than either of us had planned. "Oh, well, I better go. Bye, Deb."

"Goodnight, Joe."

The line went dead. I smiled as I put the phone down. I should have recorded that conversation, I thought. By tomorrow he'd have forgotten all about it and he'd be back to being his conceited, obnoxious self!

Chapter Eleven

Joe did come back to work on Friday, but he was not, as I'd hoped, his old, cool, confident self. He had obviously already been at the cafe for some time when I arrived, even though I was slightly early for once. All the tables had already been prepared and the condiment bottles were already full.

"Hey, you are being nice to me," I said, walking into the kitchen, where Joe was already heating the grill. "All those jobs already done. Is it boy scout good deed week or what?"

Joe would normally have grinned at that and made some smart remark. That day he didn't even look round from the grill. "I wanted to make sure all the outside things were taken care of," he said. "I just don't feel like facing people yet. I'll do the cooking today. You wait tables."

"Okay," I said, "but wouldn't it be much easier to get this over with? If you go out and act like everything is back to normal, that's how they'll react. If you keep on hiding away, they'll start making a big thing of it too."

"I don't need a lecture from you," he said shortly. "If I could act like everything was back to normal I would. Just let me handle this my way."

Customers started arriving and Joe made very sure that he stayed hidden in the kitchen.

"Is that Joe back in there?" people asked me. "How's he feeling?" I told them all that he was feeling pretty bad and I couldn't get him to come out of the kitchen yet.

We left him alone all evening, even though we were all itching to do something. When he answered me in polite monosyllables, I even wished for the return of the old Joe – the one who was always ready for a fight and answered everything with a witty putdown. I decided that maybe it was up to me to get him back on his feet again, that maybe if I got him mad enough he'd snap out of this depression.

Next time I brought in a pile of dishes I remarked casually, "I just wish someone would give the kids out there a lesson in how to dress. I think they must shop at Bargain Mart! Haven't they even heard of boutiques?"

"Uh-huh," he grunted, and went back to putting burgers on the grill. I tried again. "If only I could get Grant to come down here, he might tell you guys how to look cool. He always shops at Neiman Marcus, of course, but then you have to if you want to look right, don't you?"

"Uh-huh," Joe said again, as if he hadn't even heard me. I decided to give it up and stomped out with my next orders.

"Is he going to stay in there forever?" Art demanded, glancing towards the kitchen.

"Sure looks that way," I said. "And don't go in there – that would only make it worse. He's just decided that he doesn't want to face people yet, and there's nothing you can do about it. Believe me, I've tried. I told him Grant might be able to give him some pointers on dressing and he didn't even react!"

"Boy, he must be in a bad way," Art agreed.

"Poor Joe," Ashley sighed. "Maybe if I went in and gave him my most passionate kiss, that might give him interest in life again."

Terry spluttered into his drink. "That would make him join the Foreign Legion," he said.

"How about if we try shock therapy?" Howard asked excitedly, waving his arms and knocking napkins to the floor. "I know that works! We'll put Ashley on the floor and cover her in ketchup and say that I went berserk with a chainsaw! That should work!"

"Are you crazy?" Ashley shrieked. "I have on a thirty-dollar sweater. You are not pouring ketchup over me, not even for Joe."

"Then what are we going to do?" Howard asked. "I sure hate to see him depressed."

"Why don't we just tell him that the dumb movie didn't matter?" Terry asked.

"I've tried that a million times," I said. "He's just not listening. We have to think of something to get his self-confidence back. He used to think he was the coolest guy around and he thinks that everybody's seen him acting like a fool. We've got to make him think he's cool again."

"But how?"

"We'll have to stage something so that he can be the hero," I said.

"We could set the kitchen on fire again!" Howard suggested hopefully.

"And what if he doesn't act like a hero and the cafe burns down?" I asked. "I do not feel like putting out any more fires. One was enough for me."

"We could pretend there was some sort of emergency and yell for him to help," Ashley suggested.

"Right," Terry said. "With anyone in particular in need of help?"

"Wait," I said quickly, "Ashley's got a good idea. Let's think about it tonight, and we can pool our ideas tomorrow."

That night I lay in bed and tried to come up with a brilliant plan to make Joe feel like king of the hill again. It must be subtle, of course. Joe was no idiot, and he'd know instantly if we tried to stage something obvious. I wondered if I could get any of my friends from school to dress up as punks and then to start a fight at the cafe. Then Joe could come and sort them out and show them who was boss. The only thing wrong with that was that Joe might not respond and someone else might call the police, which my friends would not appreciate.

"Someone else's fertile mind is sure to come up with something better," I muttered to myself as I drifted off to sleep. "And there sure are some fertile minds at that cafe."

My sleep was full of weird dreams. I dreamed Howard had dressed up as a dinosaur and ripped the roof off the cafe and started to chomp the furniture, only he was really about a hundred feet tall and he started eating people. I kept yelling for Joe but he wouldn't come, and I kept hoping that Howard would not be able to breathe inside the dinosaur suit and would stop wrecking the cafe.

"This was a dumb idea," I was moaning as I woke up.

The dream left me shaken and I decided we had to plan very carefully and keep a careful eye on what people like Howard were doing. Not that I thought even *he* was capable of turning into a hundred-foot dinosaur and eating the roof of the cafe, but you never knew!

As I got out of my car at the cafe that afternoon, the first thing I saw was Howard's face, inches away from mine. I screamed and leaped back into the car before I noticed that he was not dressed as a dinosaur. He looked really surprised.

"Is something wrong?" he asked. "Do I have a zit or something?"

"No, n-nothing's wrong," I managed to stammer. "I was lost in thought and you just startled me, that's all."

"I bet you were trying to think up a good plan for Joe," he said, nodding like one of those dogs you see in the backs of cars. "But you don't have to worry, because I've come up with the perfect plan."

I wondered for a moment if he had the hundred-foot dinosaur suit folded in his backpack. "You're not thinking of dressing up as a dinosaur?" I asked hurriedly.

He looked confused. "Why would I want to do that?" he asked. "Joe would realize a dinosaur wasn't real."

"Only joking," I said with a halfhearted smile. "Of course you wouldn't be planning to eat the roof of the cafe."

"Eat the roof?" he asked. He looked at me the way other people usually looked at him: as if they were not quite sure if he was a) normal and b) not dangerous. He gave a nervous little laugh. "You're just kidding, right?"

"Right," I said. "I'm sorry. Tell me about your idea."

"I thought this out carefully," he said excitedly. "It has to be something natural, something that would really happen in a cafe. So I thought, what happens in cafes, and then it came to me. People choke!"

"Not on sodas and floats," I said. "At least, not often."

"But maybe on hamburgers," he continued. "I'll pretend to choke! You all scream and panic and Joe will come out of the kitchen, do the right first aid on me, and be a hero."

"What if he doesn't come?"

"I happen to know that he took CPR and all that stuff at school," Howard said. "So he knows what to do. I don't think Joe would sit back and let someone choke to death. I'll do a pretty good imitation of a dying person – after all, I have watched enough movie deaths by now – and you can all scream that you don't know what to do!"

"Are you sure you can make it look realistic, Howard?" I asked.

"How about this?" he said and began to clutch at his throat, while his eyes began to bulge and his face turned purple. It was horribly convincing.

"Okay, okay, you can stop now," I said hastily. "That looked very convincing. I think it might work. He may not even be suspicious. Now all we need is to clue in the others and plan a time."

Howard blinked at me through his thick glasses. "I was thinking maybe it might be better not to tell the others. You know Ashley and Art. They might blow it. They might start laughing, or Ashley might say, 'Howard, are you pretending or is this real?' "

I grinned. "That's true. Okay, Howard, we'll wait until the place fills up enough so that Joe can perform his miracle in front of witnesses. But don't sit in the corner or someone might get to you first. Sit at the front table and collapse close to the counter, all right?"

"Good thinking," Howard said.

"I just hope this works," I said, as I went into the cafe.

"I'm sure it will," Howard said. "I just knew I had to come up with something before Ashley did. She had some crazy idea in her head last night – something about staging a drowning and letting Joe save her. I kept telling her to forget it. I hope she has."

"We'll do your choking as soon as possible," I said. "Before Ashley can put any crazy ideas into action."

Howard disappeared, waiting for the cafe to open, and I went inside. Joe was already there again, working busily and hardly saying two words to me. Every time I thought of Howard's plan, I started to giggle. I had to run out of the kitchen several times so that I didn't give anything away. The cafe opened and kids started to drift in. Howard entered and sat quietly at a little table close to the kitchen. I came in with a tray of drinks and noticed the group that had moved to the table behind Howard.

"Howard, those guys look like lifeguards," I whispered. "What do we do about them?"

"Hold them back until Joe gets here," he whispered. "You fling yourself between them and me. Make out you're so distressed by my dying that you can't control yourself."

"I'm not sure I'm that good an actress," I said, giving him a sideways grin. "I'd rather wait until they've finished their drinks and gone."

The group took an age to leave. Finally they went and I noticed that there were just enough kids in the cafe. I began to play my part in the drama.

"Here's your hamburger, Howard," I said, just loud enough for other people to hear.

"Thanks, Debbie," he said. "Boy, am I starving tonight. I could swallow this in one bite."

"Don't overdo it," I muttered as I plonked the ketchup in front of him.

I hovered inside the kitchen doorway.

"Here, these orders are ready," Joe said. About the longest sentence he had spoken all day. "What are you waiting for?"

"I just need a break, okay?" I said belligerently. "I had a tough day at school. Just give me a second."

"The fries are getting cold!"

"Okay, but don't blame me if I drop from exhaustion," I muttered and swept out with the fries. I had just put them down on the table when Howard went to work. He started thrashing around, doing his famous eye-bulging routine.

"Howard!" I screamed. "What's the matter?"

"Looks like he's choking!" a kid at the next table said helpfully.

"Joe! Come quick, Howard's choking!" I screamed. "I don't know what to do!"

"You just need to do the Heimlich manoeuvre," the kid at the next table said helpfully, beginning to get up. "We learned it at school."

"It's all right. We can manage," I said, nudging him back towards his seat with my elbow.

Joe appeared from the kitchen. Howard must have been really holding his breath because his lips were beginning to turn blue.

"Joe, do something!" I screamed. Joe stood behind Howard and put his arms around his middle, then brought his fists up and back. In a few seconds Howard flopped down to the table, gasping realistically. Everyone crowded around.

"I thought I was a goner. Thanks, big guy," he panted to Joe. "I couldn't breathe."

"You saved his life!" I said, in case anyone in the room might have missed that fact.

"You okay now, buddy?" Joe asked, putting a hand on Howard's shoulder.

"I think so," Howard said. "Thanks to you."

The whole scene had gone off without a hitch. It would have been a marvellous success except that at this point the door to the cafe opened and Kelly burst in, looking even wilder than usual. "Joe, come quick! Ashley's drowning! She got swept out by a wave and you're the strongest swimmer I know!" she screamed. As she grabbed his arm, he looked more than a little stunned. "Come on, please hurry, you can save her. I know you can!"

"Ashley's drowning?" he asked, peeling off his jacket as he began to move towards the door. Before he could reach the door, Terry burst in.

"Joe, old buddy, I need your help! This guy at the gas station swallowed transmission fluid by mistake. He thought it was cherry soda. We've got to get him to the hospital in a hurry. Can you take him on your bike, Joe?"

Joe had stopped hurrying to the door and began to look from Kelly to Terry to Howard and then to me. His face flushed red with embarrassment and anger. "Nice try, guys, but you must think I'm pretty stupid," he said. Then he turned his back on us and walked back into the kitchen.

"Thanks a lot. You bozos blew the whole thing," Howard said. "Joe just saved my life not two minutes ago."

Kelly looked upset. "Well, how were we to know that other people would come up with plans, too?"

"Yeah, I thought my plan was pretty good," Terry growled. "I didn't know you guys would come up with other plans. Mine would have worked great!"

"Well, as it is, we'd better forget this whole thing," I said. "We're back to square one as far as Joe is concerned. We'll just have to let him get over this on his own."

Kelly suddenly let out another scream. "Oh, no," she squeaked. "I forgot all about Ashley. She's standing up to her armpits in the cold ocean waiting to be rescued!"

"Talk about movies being weird," I muttered as I went back to work. "Working in this cafe is crazier than any movie script could be!"

Chapter Twelve

For once I had something funny to tell Grant that night. I hadn't seen him all week, and I was feeling a little nervous about seeing him again, because I intended to refuse if he said he wanted to spend the evening working on any new speeches. So I launched straight into my account of what had happened that afternoon at the cafe. I figured he'd think it was funny, but instead he agreed with Joe.

"Poor guy. I know how he must be feeling," he said. "Nobody likes being made a fool of."

"We didn't intend to make a fool of him. We wanted to help him," I insisted. It was weird to find a situation in which Grant took Joe's side. I'd have to tell Joe about it when he was back to being his old self, I thought. Right now he'd probably say what a nice guy Grant was.

"We needed to do something," I insisted. "Joe has to snap out of this depression sometime or I'm going to be stuck with all the extra work at the cafe!"

Grant drummed his fingers on the Formica tabletop. We were drinking cappuccinos at Toni's at the mall. "Are you ... planning to keep on working at that place all summer?" he asked.

"I guess," I said. "Unless someone comes along and tells me I've won a million dollars."

"So you'll be stuck here all summer, then," he said thoughtfully.

"It looks that way," I said. "I could always go and stay with my father for a break, but I don't think I can handle that yet."

"Why, what's wrong with your father?" he asked, and I realized with a jolt that I had told Joe all about my father and his girlfriends, not Grant.

"Oh, nothing," I said. "It's just that he has no room for guests. You know how I hate sharing bathrooms."

"I agree," he said. "I don't know how I'm going to survive dorm life at Harvard. Only one bathroom to every eight students! Still, I'll be getting some practice up at the lake, I suppose."

"You're going up to your folks' cabin?"

He looked slightly embarrassed. "Yeah, a group of us are going up for a couple of weeks. You know, to relax after senior year. We're leaving right after we get back from the senior trip to Hawaii. I don't suppose you'll be able to get a couple of weeks off work to join us, will you?"

I let out a disbelieving little laugh. "I don't think my mother would exactly go along with the idea of my spending a couple of weeks with you at the lake," I said. "I take it your folks won't be there."

"Are you kidding?" he laughed easily. "What would be the point of going where my folks were? It'll just be a few senior guys and their girlfriends – and a big keg of beer. And we'll take the boat up for waterskiing. Sure you can't persuade your mom?"

"I don't think so," I said, "and I'm not sure if they could survive without me for two weeks at work right now. Mr Garbarini is coming back soon, but he'll still have to take things easy."

"Oh, that's too bad," Grant said. "It would have been fun. I'll miss you." But he didn't sound as if his heart would be breaking or as if he were about to cancel the trip because I couldn't go with him.

"Looks like we'll be hardly seeing each other this summer," I said, trying to keep my voice light. "What with Hawaii and the lake . . ."

"And Mexico," he said. "My folks are insisting I come with them to Mexico again. It's a drag but you do catch great fish down there. At least I'll look tanned and healthy to start Harvard."

I played with my napkin, folding it into neat little triangles. "It's funny to think that high school's almost over for you," I said. "Only a week and a half, and you're out."

"I can't wait," he said. "If I didn't have that dumb speech hanging over me, I'd do nothing but party for the next week. As it is, I'll survive. There's nothing much to do except sign yearbooks, and of course we've got senior cut day."

"You get to cut classes?" I asked.

"You don't get to – you just do it. Old senior tradition," Grant said. "We're all meeting for a giant beach party. Sorry I can't invite you, but it's only seniors."

"That's okay," I said. "I don't really like giant beach parties anyway."

"Yeah, and you know how crazy people act when they're

almost out of high school," he said quickly. "I don't know if I'm too thrilled about a day of volleyball and ultimate Frisbee. They don't even, let you drink on the beach, so it will be all wholesome fun!"

"Which beach is it?" I asked. "I might drop by on my way to work, if that's okay. Or will it all be over by then?"

"Rockley, I guess," he said, "but it will probably be over."

"I get the feeling you'd rather I didn't stop by," I said. "Can't they bend the seniors-only rule for a few minutes?"

"You can come if you really want to," he said, but he looked away from me. "It's just that you might feel a little . . . out of it, that's all."

"So you're saying you don't want me to come?" I demanded.

"No, I didn't say that at all. You're very welcome to come – if you want to watch a bunch of seniors acting crazy."

"I only said I might stop by," I said sharply. "I wasn't planning to cut school with you, but if you'd rather I didn't—"

"No, no. Come if you want to," he insisted.

"Just say if you'd rather I didn't."

He drummed his fingers on the table. "Look, Debbie, if you'd like to come for a little while and you think you'd enjoy it, that's fine with me. I'd like to have you there. Okay? How many more times do I have to say it?"

"Fine," I muttered. "Okay."

"Let's drop the subject, all right?" Grant said. "Because I still need to talk to you about this speech. Mr Fischer – you know, the government teacher – doesn't like the way the pan about selecting colleges reads. He asked me to rewrite it.

Couldn't you liven it up for me? Right now it's all so boring. Can we go back to my house and work on it?"

"I don't know how my mother could possibly worry about my being up at the lake with you," I quipped. "The only thing you'd try to get me to do in two weeks is write your papers for your first year at Harvard for you – injecting suitable humour into all of them, of course."

"If you don't want to help me," Grant said, looking like a little boy whose friend won't play the game he wants, "that's fine, I suppose. I thought you might have enjoyed being part of a valedictory speech, that's all. I thought you'd be proud to see me up there and to hear your jokes read out to thousands of people."

It was on the tip of my tongue to say what Joe had said, to ask if he intended to give me credit in front of all those people for my parts of the speech. But I bit the words back at the last moment. It was Grant's last week of school, after all, and it wasn't really fair of me to spoil it for him. So I suffered through an evening of trying to make rejection by Ivy League colleges a humorous topic and felt totally drained by the time I got home. My mother was asleep on the sofa when I let myself in. She looked so young lying there that I tiptoed over to her and gave her a little kiss on the cheek.

She woke with a start and focused on my face for a long moment before she smiled. "Oh, did I doze off?" she asked. "I was watching such an interesting programme on TV, about the breeding habits of the whooping crane."

"Were you waiting up for me?" I asked.

"Of course not, dear. I don't worry when you're out with Grant."

Of course not, you've got nothing to worry about, I thought grimly, *except for Grant draining my brain for his crummy speeches!*

My mother stretched luxuriantly, like a cat, and got to her feet. "Heavens, is that the time? I was so exhausted. We must have walked for miles today to reach the logging site, and the ground was so muddy, my legs felt like jelly by the time we got home." She plumped the pillows on the couch, revealing that my former mother, the one from my childhood, had not totally disappeared. "So did you have a nice evening, dear?" she asked.

"Wonderful, if you call working on one joke for two hours fascinating," I said. "We polished Grant's speech, which is all we have done on dates for the last couple of years, it seems."

"Oh, dear," she said with a sigh. "Are things not going too well between Grant and you?"

"Oh, they're going just fine as far as he's concerned," I said. "It's just that I get the feeling that he only wants me around when it's convenient to him. Sometimes I think I don't matter at all to him . . . not really." I perched on the arm of the sofa, taking care not to disturb the pillows Mom had already straightened. "In fact, sometimes I get the feeling that I don't really matter to anyone. If I disappeared tomorrow a few people would be annoyed because I wasn't there to wipe tables or to write speeches or to eat lunch with, but nobody would be heartbroken."

"Of course they would, you donkey," she said. She reached up and pulled me down beside her, slipping her arm around me. "I would, for one thing. So would your father, even though he's a trifle preoccupied with his own life at the moment. He loves you to pieces and so do I."

"Hmmm," I said, because I didn't want to open that can of worms again. "So – my parents care about me. Big deal. Parents have to love their kids – even mother skunks defend their babies to the death!"

Mom laughed and hugged me hard. "Thanks for comparing me to a mother skunk," she said, "but that makes you a little skunk, doesn't it?"

I wriggled away. "It's not funny, Mom," I said.

"I know it's not, darling," she said softly. "Growing up is never easy, and you've had an especially tough year—"

"You can say that again," I interrupted.

"But everyone goes through times when they feel they don't matter," she said. "It's all part of learning who you are and where you fit in. Maybe you've outgrown your friends, or they've outgrown you – it happens, you know. Maybe deep down you're just not the same as the people you're hanging around with."

"That's sure true," I said. "I feel like I don't fit in anywhere right now."

She patted my knee as she got up from the sofa. "Maybe that's because you haven't found your proper niche in life," my mother said, taking a coffee cup over to the sink and washing it. "I felt the same until I got involved with my conservation group. You need to get out and meet more people. Maybe you'd like to come with us some weekend. I'm sure they wouldn't mind that you're not at the college, and at least you'd feel you were doing some good for our planet."

"Er, thanks, Mom. I'll think about it," I said, "but right now I'm super-tired. I'm going to bed."

I kissed her on the cheek and went back to my room, trying to ignore the big empty ache that was growing inside me. I didn't want her to tell me about saving our planet. I wanted her to tell me that she'd always be there to take care of me. And I wanted Grant to say that I mattered to him more than going to a lake and that the senior party wouldn't be the same without me. I undressed and curled into a little tight ball. Soon Grant would be gone for the summer and then he'd go off to college. My mother would be made president of the Save the Everything league and start flying round the world to save polar bears and snowmen, my father would marry one of the bikini cuties he'd been dating since the divorce and have hundreds of new children he'd like better than me, and I'd be out in the cold, all alone. *She's right,* I thought unhappily, *I don't truly belong anywhere.*

Then a thought came to me, making my eyes jerk wide open again, staring at the ceiling. I had felt annoyed when Grant told me he was going to be away most of the summer. And my pride had been hurt because he'd obviously chosen the lake and his friends over me. But I certainly wasn't heartbroken. Could it be that Grant had become just a habit for me? I had seen my friends fall in love at school. They walked around with silly grins on their faces and murmured the guy's name over and over. I might have done that a year earlier, when Grant and I first started going together, but it had been a long time since I'd murmured his name with a silly grin on my face.

In fact, now that I thought about it, my main feeling about Grant's absence was relief. I wouldn't have to live up to being Grant's perfect girlfriend. I wouldn't have to watch what I said to his friends or stand beside him with my fake doll's smile while he had his picture taken.

Of course, as soon as these thoughts surfaced, I started to feel really uneasy. Grant annoyed me sometimes with his chauvinistic attitudes, but I didn't want to break up with him, did I? Getting a boyfriend, especially a popular boyfriend, was one of the major objectives of high school, wasn't it? The realization that I didn't want a boyfriend any more just added to the craziness round me already: my formerly shy mother advising me to meet more people; Joe, no longer Mr Macho, hiding in the kitchen afraid to face anyone. And me? What did I want? When I thought about that, I just wasn't sure. I didn't even know who I was at all. Finally I drifted into unsettled sleep.

Chapter Thirteen

I was not looking forward to the day ahead of me as I pulled up outside the Heartbreak Cafe on Sunday morning. For one thing, I had not slept well. For another, they were filming right behind the cafe again, and the whole area was roped off while the famous Hollywood stuntman did his famous Hollywood stunts with his high-powered motorcycle. I could hear it revving to a high-pitched scream as I got out of the car, and I noticed the admiring crowds perched on our back fence to get a better view.

Joe's going to be thrilled about this! I thought, taking a deep breath before I entered the cafe.

He was cleaning up in the kitchen and acknowledged my presence with only a nod.

"Good morning," I said cheerfully, taking my uniform out of the closet and hanging up my purse there.

"Humpph!" he answered.

"I can see this is going to be another fun-filled day of laughter and sunshine," I said sweetly. "You might at least try to be pleasant to me."

He turned to look at me coldly. "I suppose that was all your idea yesterday," he said. "You just can't stop interfering, can you? You think that being from a superior planet makes you better than the rest of us, gives you the right to butt in. First it was trying to turn this cafe into a copy of those fancy places down on the beach – calamari and hanging plants, wasn't it? And now I bet you thought you'd get poor old Joe snapped out of his mood in a couple of seconds, right?"

"Wrong," I said, eyeing him equally coldly. We glared at each other in silence. "As a matter of fact, Mr Know-it-all," I said, "I had nothing to do with what happened yesterday, except to bring Howard the hamburger he choked on. The choking was all his idea, and apparently Ashley and Terry had the same sort of thoughts. I helped but I wasn't the instigator."

"Oh," he said. "I suppose that makes sense. You were probably delighted to see me look like a fool. It's the first chance you've ever had to get the better of me."

"If I'd wanted to get the better of you," I said, my voice rising dangerously, "I could have had a field day! I could have told every customer who came in here exactly what happened on that movie set. I could have told them how you were all prepared to pack up for Hollywood. I could even have told Wendy. But I didn't, and if you really want to know the truth, I hate seeing you like this. I'm disgusted by the way you are wallowing in self-pity."

"I am not wallowing!" he said angrily. "I've just taken a kick in the guts, that's all."

"What's so terrible about that?" I demanded. "One little embarrassing moment isn't the end of your life, you know."

"It feels like it to me," he said. "I've been humiliated in front of everyone I know. They won't ever think I'm cool again."

"Baloney!" I snapped. "They all put themselves out for you yesterday. Ashley went and stood in that cold ocean and even got her hair wet waiting to pretend to drown. Howard nearly really choked to death to look realistic for you. They didn't mind making fools of themselves for you, did they?"

He didn't answer but went back to rinsing dishes.

"You just don't understand what it was like for me," he said quietly. "I can't explain it."

"I understand how you felt," I said. "I felt pretty much the same when I ran to my father because I thought he'd want me, and instead he had a pretty young woman there. I felt so rejected and scared and angry … and remember what you said that day? You told me that life is tough sometimes, and I'd better get used to it. Maybe you should follow your own advice."

"I'm trying to," he muttered. "Just give me time."

"Okay, Joe, I'll give you time," I said quietly, "but just remember that your friends won't keep on trying forever. If you keep shutting people out, in the end they'll give up on you."

"I guess you're right," he said.

"Could you say that again?" I asked, hope rising. "That's twice you've admitted I was right in the past few days. If I make it a third time, do I get a prize?"

"A night with me?" he asked, with just a glimmer of his former smile.

"And don't tell me – the second prize is two nights with Grant, right?" I asked, and we both grinned.

I got down to work then, but I sensed that Joe really was

trying to make an effort and that he appreciated having me in the kitchen beside him. Fortunately it was a slow day for the cafe since most of the lunchtime crowd was still watching the movie being shot. By silent agreement neither Joe nor I mentioned the movie or the loud rumble of a motorcycle engine right outside our kitchen window.

By mid-afternoon the regulars began to wander in, one by one. Art and Josh came in, propping surfboards up against the wall. Howard settled himself at the table in the corner. Kelly came in and joined him.

"Where's Ashley?" I asked as I came to take their orders. "Is she still watching the movie? Shouldn't somebody be keeping an eye on her – you know that she's liable to fling herself in front of Troy Heller's car or walk across the set in a bikini!"

"They've finished shooting for the day," Kelly said. "They did all the motorcycle shots this morning. Ashley was there then. I don't know where she went after that."

"Ashley?" Art called from his table. "She went off with Harris Barclay – didn't she tell you?"

"Harris Barclay?" I asked. "Ashley went off where with him?"

"He said something about going back to his motel room," Art said casually.

"His motel room?" I blurted out. "What for?"

Art grinned. "He said something about some pictures, I think."

"Why, that little creep," Kelly burst out. "I always thought that Barclay guy was a slimy toad. Now he's lured Ashley back to his room. You always read about that sort of thing happening in movies, don't you?"

I was staring at Art in disbelief. "You l-let Ashley go b-back to Harris Barclay's motel room?" I stammered.

Art looked surprised. "Yeah, why not? What she does is her business."

"But Art," I said, "you know Ashley. The way she looks and the way she really is . . . well, you know they're two completely different things. You know she's not really the sort of girl Harris Barclay obviously thinks she is."

"She said she'd do anything to get into movies," Howard commented, peering worriedly through his thick glasses. "I guess she really meant it."

"But it won't get her into movies!" I exclaimed angrily. "Harris Barclay is just using her. You know that!" I turned to Art, who was now looking rather stunned and guilty after my outburst. "How long ago was this?"

Art shrugged and looked at Josh. "About half an hour ago, maybe, right, Josh?"

Josh frowned. "Yeah, we left when they started taking down the lights and things. We went over to check out the waves, but they weren't good enough so we came over here. Must have been half an hour or so."

"We've got to do something," I exclaimed. "We'll go over to the motel and get her out of there! I'd never have suspected Harris Barclay of being like that . . . He hasn't seemed interested in any of the girls here, has he?"

"It's always the quiet ones who are worst," Kelly said knowingly. "They're always the ones you see on the news who cut up bodies and bury them in the backyard and the neighbours always say what nice quiet people they were."

Now that Kelly mentioned it, there was something not quite normal about Harris Barclay's fishy stare, I thought. We had to get Ashley out of there, whether she liked it or not.

"We've got to go rescue her," I said. "Will you come, Art?"

"Not me," he said. "I'm not into breaking down motel doors. It's her business, like I said."

"I'll come," Howard said excitedly. "I can take him on – I know karate!"

I took a quick look at Howard. If it came to a fight, even another nerd like Harris could blow him away. It really needed someone tough-looking … like Joe. I ran into the kitchen.

"Joe, we need your help!" I said. "Come quick."

He looked up suspiciously. "Not another choking," he said. "Or is it drowning today?"

"I'm serious," I said. "It's Ashley. She went off to Harris Barclay's motel with him. You know how she looks, but she's so naive really. We've got to get her out of there."

He still looked suspicious. "Are you sure this isn't another little plan – it's better than yesterday's, I'll admit—"

"Look, I don't have time to argue with you," I said. "If you're not coming, I'm going on my own. I care about Ashley and I don't want her to do anything dumb just because she's starstruck."

I started to run out of the kitchen again. "Looks like it's just you and me, Howard," I called. "Come on, we'll go in my car."

"You can't send Howard to rescue anyone!" Joe shouted,

haha too true

right behind me. He looked hard at me. "If you're making this up and it's another little plan for me . . ." He didn't finish the sentence.

"I'm not making anything up," I said. He ran over to his bike. "Jump on," he said. I climbed on behind him. "Howard, keep an eye on the cafe."

"Do you know which motel?" I asked.

"The movie crew's staying up at the Blue Lagoon," Joe shouted back.

The bike roared to life. I was conscious of incredible speed and I clung tightly to Joe. Pavement flashed past us as we began to snake up the canyon. We took bends at impossible angles. Wind tore at my hair and clothing and I could feel my heart thumping against Joe's back. After a few minutes I stopped feeling scared and exhilaration took over. It was almost like flying. I'd driven fast in Grant's sports car, but I'd never felt like this. The closeness of the roar, the smell of shrubs growing from the canyon walls, the warmth of the wind – all of my senses came awake at once. And added to the other sensations was the close warmness of Joe's back, of my arms round him . . .

He must have realized I was clutching him tightly because at the end of the ride, as we screeched to a halt in the Blue Lagoon parking lot, he turned to smile at me over his shoulder. "You see, you didn't fall off, did you?" he asked.

I climbed down, shakily. My knees didn't want to obey me and I tried to walk briskly towards the front desk without staggering.

"Do you think they'll tell us which room?" I asked.

Joe was looking round. He saw a maid pushing a cart of laundry along the walkway and ran over to her. After a short exchange he ran back to me. "She saw a girl with a lot of hair going into one-oh-four," he said. "Come on." He took my hand as if it was the most natural thing in the world.

Room 104 was luckily around the side of the building so that we didn't have to hammer on the door in full view of the world. Joe banged loudly on the door.

"Harris Barclay?" he demanded.

"Yes?" a decidedly suspicious voice answered back.

"Come on, open up in there before we call the police," Joe shouted. "We know you've got a girl in there."

The door opened, almost immediately, and Harris Barclay's frightened face looked out. It took him a moment to register who we were.

"You've got a girl in there, one of our friends," Joe said menacingly. "We've come to get her!"

"Oh, thank heavens," Harris Barclay said. "You don't know how glad I am to see you!"

He stood aside to reveal Ashley, draped over his bed. She looked up as we came in.

"What are you doing here?" she demanded. "I almost had him convinced—"

"What is going on here exactly?" I asked, looking first at Joe, then at Barclay.

Harris Barclay sat back on a chair, mopping his forehead. "It's all been a nightmare, a horrible nightmare," he whispered. "She kept pestering me for a photo of Troy. I put her off by saying they were back at my motel room. Well, I arrived here and there she was! I gave her the picture of Troy, but she wouldn't go! Then she started telling me how she should be in movies and I had to watch her act and then she, er, made a pass at me! I didn't know what to do." Harris Barclay's face was bright scarlet with embarrassment. "I kept telling her to stop. I was terrified that someone would hear her. How would that have looked – a young girl in my room. And think of the bad publicity for the movie!"

Joe walked over to Ashley and looked down at her severely. "Is this true, Ashley?" he demanded.

Ashley slid silently from the bed. "You had to spoil my one chance, didn't you?" she murmured. "I had to get into the movie somehow, and I might have made him hire me if you hadn't come along."

"Get your things," Joe said. "You're going home."

"Spoilsport," Ashley muttered. "I don't even like you any more, Joe Garbarini!"

"You are just lucky that Mr Barclay is a nice guy," Joe said firmly. He took her arm and led her outside. "Sorry about that," he called back to Barclay. "We'll keep a better eye on her in the future."

Harris Barclay followed us to the door. "Thank you so much," he said. "I'm grateful."

The door closed behind us.

"I'll drive her back to the cafe first, then I'll come get you, okay?" Joe asked.

"I don't want to go back to the cafe," Ashley said defiantly.

I took her arm. "Ashley, I don't think you realize what could have happened to you! Girls go to guys' motel rooms for one reason only. Would you really have been prepared to sleep with a strange man just for the chance of getting into a movie?"

Ashley looked less defiant. "I didn't really intend to let him get that far," she said. "I just wanted him to see how sexy I could be."

"And then what?" I asked. "Who did you think was going to come when you yelled for help?"

"I, er, I don't know," she said. "I could have handled it."

"No, you couldn't," Joe said fiercely. "Even a wimp like Barclay is stronger than you. You just thank your stars that he's a nice guy. Really, Ashley, you've done some pretty stupid things in your time, but this was the most stupid!"

Suddenly her defiance disappeared like a popped bubble. She gave a big sigh. "You don't know what it's like, do you?" she asked, looking first at me and then at Joe. "You don't know what it's like being a total nobody. Nobody in the world thinks you're anything special, nobody notices you, you're not good at anything. Well, I just had a stupid dream, I guess. I dreamed that maybe I was a good actress, and all I wanted was the chance to prove it."

I had a sudden urge to hug her. She looked so depressed, so lost. "Look, Ashley," I said quietly. "If you really want to be an actress, you have to do it properly: study, go to college, work hard. People being discovered on the streets or in cafes only happens in movies or sensational magazines, not real life."

"And we all think we're nobody special some of the time," Joe added. "Even the most famous people in the world have times when they think they're ugly or dumb or unloved. Even

I just thought—" He broke off and turned away, walking over to his bike.

I touched her arm lightly. "Go on, Joe's waiting!"

I watched them both fondly as they disappeared down the hill, still amazed at how close Joe had come to confessing that he had felt all the things Ashley felt. Maybe this would be a turning point for him. I only hoped he wasn't mad at me that this wasn't really a rescue. And I hoped he didn't think I set this one up.

It didn't seem like any time at all before Joe's bike appeared again up the hill.

"Good deed for the day done, I guess," he said.

I wiggled my toes uneasily in my sandals. "Look, Joe. I'm sorry it didn't turn out to be a great rescue."

"Are you kidding?" he asked, a big grin spreading across his face. "We saved Harris from a fate worse than death, didn't we?"

"Maybe . . ." I said, laughing.

"I wasn't talking about that!" he answered. "I meant Ashley's acting!"

I climbed on to the bike behind him, and, although I was not scared this time, I still wrapped my arms round his waist tightly.

Chapter Fourteen

I'd almost forgotten about senior cut day and I probably would never have gone to the party that evening if I hadn't been in the girls' bathroom at school when Minda McSweeney walked in. Minda was one of those seniors who acted like she was the most important person in the world. She was a cheerleader and popular and pretty. I had also seen the other side of her when her group came into the Heartbreak once and treated me like dirt just because I was the waitress. I was in one of the stalls when she walked in.

"Hey, Minda, what are you doing here? It's senior cut day, isn't it?" a surprised voice asked. It sounded like Diana Fisher, a junior. I paused inside the stall with my hand on the door.

"I know," Minda said, "but that creepy Mr Bliese said he was giving me an F in chemistry if I didn't show up for the rest of the semester, and my parents would kill me if I didn't graduate. I wouldn't be able to go on the graduation trip to Hawaii." Then she laughed, as if the whole thing were a huge joke.

"So he made you be here on senior cut day?" Diana asked. "Boy, what a jerk. You must be the only senior in school."

"There are a few of us – all Mr Bliese's prisoners," Minda said. "But don't worry. I have chemistry third period and I plan to split immediately after that. Besides, that beach party thing is nothing. Who wants to play volleyball all day? The real party doesn't start until this evening."

"Really? There's going to be another party?"

"Uh-huh. Don't blab it around because we don't want too many people there, but my folks have a beach cottage at Chelsea Cove – you know, just down from Rockley. And they're letting me have a party there with my friends. It's great because the cops stop you if you drink on the beach, but you can do what you like in our backyard, which also happens to be beach!"

"Sounds great," Diana said. "I can't wait to be a senior."

"Come if you want," Minda said. "A few juniors are coming . . ."

There was a pause and the sound of hair being brushed. Then: "Did you invite Debbie Lesley, by any chance?"

Laughter. "Now why would I want to do a thing like that?" Another pause. "Actually, it doesn't matter too much. I think Grant's getting tired of her anyway. It's just hard to break things off sometimes. Believe me, I know. I've been trying to get rid of Teddy all year, but every time I'm just about to tell him to get lost, there's another prom or something I need a partner for. Boys are such a drag, aren't they?"

The two voices faded away and I heard the door swing shut behind them. I came out slowly and stood looking at myself in the mirror. So Minda was out to get Grant – my Grant. I found myself shivering, even though it wasn't that cold in the bathroom. He might have been annoying me recently, but I hadn't seriously considered breaking up with Grant. And I

yes you had. You only want him now because another girl shown interest in him too.

certainly hadn't worried about losing him to somebody else. Minda was one of the most gorgeous girls in the school, and she was pretty sophisticated, too. What chance did I have against someone like that?

I began to pace up and down the empty room, my shoes making neat little tapping noises on the tile, like a clock ticking. The more I thought about it, the more desirable Grant seemed. I had the most outstanding guy in the school for a boyfriend, and I loved the feeling I got when I climbed into his car beside him or when he held my hand in the halls. I imagined how horrible and embarrassing it would be to watch Minda with him instead of me, to hear the whispers: "Yes, he dumped Debbie for Minda, you know."

"No way!" I said out loud, and the words echoed back from the tiled walls much louder than I intended. Minda was not going to get Grant without a fight! I was going to crash that senior party and make sure she didn't get near him.

It was about time I stuck up for my own rights, I thought. Everyone seemed to think they could walk all over me. It was about time I showed them they were wrong. If Grant really wasn't interested in Minda, he'd be glad to have me around that evening to keep Minda away from him. And if he was interested, I couldn't wait to see his face when I showed up!

Of course, my fighting words evaporated by the end of the day and about every ten minutes I changed my mind about going or not going. After all, it was a senior party I was crashing. I imagined people looking up and saying, "What are you doing here? You're only a junior." I'm not normally a pushy sort of person who could brush off stares and smart remarks, but every time I decided not to go, I had to remind myself that I might lose Grant forever. Then I reminded myself that boyfriends like Grant didn't come along more than once in a lifetime and it seemed that any risk was worth taking to keep Minda away from him.

No. What does she mean 'Boyfriends like Grant'? He's awful (a ne

By evening I was a bundle of nerves. Several other unsettling thoughts had crept into my mind, 'thoughts like, *What if Grant likes her better than me? What if he's looking for an excuse to break up?* Every time I had thoughts like that, I almost decided not to go again. Maybe it would be better to put off confronting Grant.

Maybe I didn't even want to know where I stood with him.

Too bad that Joe had actually given me the evening off for once. Working at the cafe would have been a perfect excuse to get out of confronting Grant. As it was, I had no excuse. My mother arrived home with the usual crowd of followers, who were now smart enough to show up at dinnertime, and I was not going to be brought into a planning session on saving the salt marsh mouse. So I put on my white miniskirt and my favourite pink-and-white striped blouse, which Grant had once said made me look sexy, and drove in the direction of the beach.

I didn't have to worry about finding out which cottage was Minda's. I could hear the noise coming from behind it as I cruised up and down the street looking for a parking space. They were all taken and I had to park almost back in Rockley, which was good because it made me fighting mad again. I decided to approach the party from the beach because I didn't have the nerve to walk up to the front of Minda's cottage and ring the doorbell. What if she opened it and told me I wasn't invited? So it made more sense to just happen to be walking along the beach looking for Grant, and just happen to wander into Minda's backyard and find him there.

The only thing wrong with this was that the tide was up and it was super-tiring walking over all that soft sand. By the time I reached the cottage and saw the outlines of milling figures outside it, I was not looking or feeling as fresh and sexy as I had hoped. Strands of my hair were sticking to my forehead and my legs were all sandy and I was a little out of breath. I stood in the darkness, out of sight of the party, getting my breath back and preparing to make a good entrance. Raised voices and laughter floated across to me over the booming of the surf. Someone had built a fire in the sand and the black silhouettes around it looked like tribal dancers as they moved through the firelight. I had often felt like an outsider in my life, but never more than that moment, watching those shadows.

"Coward," I said to myself. "What have you got to lose? Either Grant's pleased to see you or he isn't. Either way you'll know how he really feels." I forced myself to walk those last steps over the dunes to the party.

I didn't spot him right away. There were a lot of people in Minda's backyard, some spilling out on to the public beach beyond. A barbecue was going and the drifting smells made my stomach growl. A crowd of kids was apparently waiting for hamburgers, hopefully holding paper plates and napkins. Everyone I looked at seemed to be a senior, and I almost decided to melt back on to the beach again when I heard Grant's voice. His voice was unusually strong and clear and easy to pick out from the crowd.

"And then the clerk says, 'Sorry, don't know about botany. I've only got a degree in economies'." This was greeted with a roar of laughter.

I recognized the joke as well as his voice. It was one of the ones I had given him. I made my way towards the voice.

"Oh, that's great," one of the other guys said. "Those graduation ceremonies are *sooo* boring. That should liven things up!"

"I've got a few more included in the speech," Grant said. "I don't want to come across like a professor! I'm even including one about two dropouts at the unemployment office." And he went on to tell another of my jokes.

"Where did you come up with all these?" a girl asked.

"You like them? You think they fit?" Grant sounded nervous.

"I think they're terrific. They show a good sense of humour."

Grant replied modestly, "Well, I don't think a valedictory speech should be too stuffy, you know. I had to come up with one or two funny parts – for all the morons in the audience who can't follow the statistics!"

More laughter. I felt my cheeks burning even though I was not standing that close to the fire. I pushed my way through the crowd.

"Oh, there you are, Grant, I've been looking for you," I said sweetly, slipping my arm through his.

I saw him swallow hard and his eyes darted nervously

from side to side. "Oh, Debbie … er, hi," he said. "I didn't think you'd show up."

"You did tell me I was welcome to stop by if I wanted to come," I said. I felt calm and cold as steel inside – and for the first time in our relationship I wasn't in awe of Grant or afraid of doing something wrong. This time I knew I had the upper hand and I was almost enjoying it.

He forced his best campaign smile. "Of course I wanted you to come," he said. "Here, let's get you a drink." He led me across to a long picnic table. "Most of the guys are drinking beer," he said, "but there's champagne. I expect you'll only want a soda, right?"

I was already extending a glass towards a guy holding a dark green bottle. "Sure, champagne, why not?" I asked as he filled it. I took a sip. It was bubbly and tickled my nose – and it didn't taste half bad. "Good champagne," I said, and drained the glass.

"Hey, go easy," Grant said as I held my glass out to be refilled. "That's not Seven-Up, you know."

"You're always telling me to loosen up at parties," I reminded him. "This is a senior party, right? And in a couple of days I'll be a senior. I'm growing up." I eyed him provocatively over the rim of my glass.

He looked round again, as if he expected someone to be watching him over his shoulder. "I, er, was in line for a hamburger," he said. "I'd better go see if Peter saved my place. Come on over."

"I think I'll mingle first," I said, imitating all those bored country club women who used to come to my parents' parties.

I eased my way through the crowd. The champagne was already beginning to work. I could feel it tingling through my body, making me feel light and more relaxed. Nobody seemed to recognize me or speak to me. I felt like a phantom, drifting among groups, too chicken to join one of them.

Then at last I came on a group of girls with Minda in it. I was looking forward to seeing her face, and I started to grin in anticipation.

"Sounds like fun," someone was saying. "Who else is going to be there?"

"Only a few of us – about ten, I think," Minda answered. "And your folks don't mind?"

"My folks will be safely in Europe," she said, and laughed. "Besides, I'm eighteen now. I can officially do what I want."

"Is it only seniors going?" another voice asked. Minda laughed again. "Meaning will Grant be unaccompanied? Actually, the whole thing was his idea. I guess after a year with the little princess, he's decided to look for more adult company!"

"This cabin, is it real rustic?"

Again I heard Minda's high, giggling laugh. "It has plenty of cosy little corners, if that's what you want to know!"

I pushed my way back through the crowd. I had heard all I wanted to hear. Reason told me to go straight home, but I found myself back at the champagne table with an empty glass. Did Grant really think about me like that? I didn't think I'd been the one who had been cold or hesitant. Of course, there had been the time when my folks refused to let me go to the lake with him, but that was understandable, wasn't it? Most normal parents wouldn't let a sixteen-year-old daughter spend a weekend at a lake cabin alone with a boy – except for Minda's parents, of course. But then, Minda was eighteen, I reminded myself. That made a difference. I drank the champagne that had miraculously appeared in my glass. Snatches of conversation floated around me.

"And he's selling the Corvette. I told him to buy a Porsche instead. I mean, American cars are just not in these days."

"And when we get to Rome . . ."

"What's your father giving you for graduation? Mine said that since I already had the car and the trip to Europe, there was nothing left to give, so I told him cash would do nicely."

"She thinks she looks so hot, but she's really tacky. That prom dress was only rented, you know."

"You're kidding? Boy, what nerve!"

"She's a bitch anyway. I don't know why she ever thought I liked her."

I turned away from the last group, almost scared that I'd hear myself ripped to shreds yet again, and grabbed a couple of potato chips from a nearby bowl. I suddenly remembered that I hadn't eaten since lunch, and I was now feeling distinctly weird – almost as if I were outside my body, watching everything in slow motion. I found Grant just coming away from the barbecue with a large hamburger on his plate.

"Oh, Grant, here I am," I said, tottering over to him. "Did you miss me?" I pressed myself up against him, my lips aiming for his mouth.

"Hey, Debbie, cut it out," he said, half laughing. "You've been drinking."

"Right. You always kept telling me that I'd have more fun if I tried it and you know, you were right. It makes me feel all warm inside. Let's leave these people and go down on the dunes, okay?"

"But I've just got a hamburger," he said. "I want to eat it while it's hot. And I really think you should eat something too. It's not a great idea to drink too much champagne without food."

"But I'm not hungry," I said. "Don't you think I'm sexy? Is that why you didn't want to take me to the lake with you, because I'm not sexy?"

"Debbie!" he hissed. "We're in the middle of a crowd. We'll talk about this later."

"But I want to know," I insisted. "Don't you want to ... you know?"

"Debbie!" He sounded shocked. "If you must know, I didn't invite you to the lake because I knew you wouldn't be allowed to come. I didn't want to put pressure on you, okay? Now let's drop the subject and for heaven's sake let me eat my hamburger."

"All right, Grant," I said. "I'll just go find myself some more of that nice champagne. I like the way it tickles my nose ..."

"I think you've had enough," he said. "Why don't you find somewhere to sit for a while ... get yourself something to eat ..."

He was right, I thought. Getting drunk wasn't bad. You felt like you were floating. It was a nice feeling ... you didn't have to worry about a thing any more. No more worries … just floating.

The next glass slipped down without even tickling my nose, but it made me hiccough, causing people to turn and stare at me. I didn't care. I just giggled. Then I went to find Grant again.

I found him leaning against the cottage wall. He wasn't alone. Minda had her arms draped round his neck and was looking up into his face, talking and smiling. Suddenly the champagne bubble popped. I strode over to them.

"What do you think you are doing with my boyfriend?" I demanded. "Get your slimy hands off him – he's mine!"

Minda's arms slid down, away from Grant's neck. "Well … sorry," she said, eyeing me with interest, "but it is my party and I don't remember inviting you."

"That's because you're trying every lowdown trick there is to steal my guy," I said. "Just because you're not pretty or smart enough to win him without stooping to—"

Grant stepped between us and grabbed my arm. "Hey, Debbie, cut it out," he said. "Minda was just being friendly. Now please cool it, will you?" He turned back to Minda. "She's had too much champagne, I'm afraid. She's not used to drinking."

"I can see that," Minda said, giving me an amused sneer. "Maybe we should find her somewhere to sleep it off."

"You only want me out of the way so you can get your hands on Grant," I yelled. "Don't think I can't see right through you."

"Debbie!" Grant said, attempting to hold me as I made a

lunge at Minda.

"Let go of me," I shouted. "Let me at her. I'll squash her like the little worm she is. And don't think I can't. I've got muscles, you know – muscles from lifting hundreds and hundreds of plates in that cafe you despise so much."

I wrestled myself free. Minda took a nervous step backwards. Grant grabbed me again and this time held me very firmly.

"Debbie, please behave yourself," he whispered. "These are my friends. You're embarrassing me."

"Didn't anyone ever think that you might be embarrassing me?" I demanded. "What about telling my jokes and sneaking off with Minda – do you think I enjoy that? In fact, I can't even remember the last time I had fun with you. If Minda has as much fun with you up at the lake as I've had recently, she'll die of boredom!"

Grant half carried me across the lawn. "Debbie, quiet down," he was saying. "We'll find you somewhere to rest and Minda will get you some black coffee. You've just had too much champagne, that's all."

"That's not all," I shouted to anyone who would listen. "I don't even enjoy being with you and I haven't had too much champagne. I only stuck around because I liked being famous, but now that you've won all the awards in the world I can tell everyone that you're boring, boring, boring!"

Grant hauled me into the house like a sack of potatoes. I closed my eyes and the world spun crazily. Suddenly I didn't feel like fighting any more. I felt horribly sick and not even sure which planet I was on. Every time I opened my eyes, people seemed to be laughing at me – horrible mean faces, all laughing. I began to feel scared.

"Grant," I pleaded. "Take me home. I want to go home."

"Now now, Debbie," he said patiently. "I don't want to leave the party now. Why don't you just try to sleep, and then you'll feel much better – you'll see."

"I can't sleep," I said. "Every time I close my eyes the world turns upside down."

"We'll get you some coffee, then you'll feel better," he said. He dumped me on to a sofa in a small back room. "There, you'll be fine in here."

"Don't go, Grant! I don't want to be left alone," I said, feeling the panic rising. "Please. I want to go home. I want to be in my own bed, Grant. Please take me home."

"Later, Debbie. Just be a good girl for a while and I'll drive you home later."

"Then I'll drive myself home now," I said, struggling to get to my feet again.

"You'll do no such thing," he said firmly. "You're not in any condition to drive. Just lie there until I come and get you. Understand?"

"Don't leave me here alone," I pleaded. "Everything's swinging round again."

"I'll be back. Just relax," he said, and closed the door behind me.

"You don't care about me at all," I called after him. "If you cared about me, you'd drive me home. You want to be with Minda. Okay, see if I care. I'll just drive myself home instead. See how you feel when you come back and find I've gone!"

Seriously? He just left her there? She definitly needs to get rid of him ASAP.

Then I got unsteadily to my feet and staggered out through the front door, on to the darkened street, and into the night.

Chapter Fifteen

The cold wind blowing off the ocean brought me to my senses. I found myself standing in a dark street with no idea where I was or where I had left my car. I didn't know if I'd turned left or right after I left Minda's cottage or where a main road was or where I'd find an all-night store or a phone. I was wide awake enough to realize that it was not smart to be completely alone on a dark back street in an unknown place. In my twisted logic, I decided to find the ocean – then I could at least walk back along the beach. I broke into a run, pulling my thin blouse tighter around me as I ran. I tried to remember where I had left my car. I seemed to remember a large pine tree nearby and scanned the area for pines. In the distance I heard the rumble of a passing car, and I headed towards it. The street went on and on. I began to wonder if I was really still lying on a couch in Minda's cottage and this was just a hallucination. Surely no streets in real life were as long as this!

Then, without warning, the street turned a corner and I came out into a well-lit area of little stores and restaurants. Now all I had to do was find a pay phone and call my mother to come and get me. Even through the fuzz inside my head I could tell that it was not going to sound too good telling her that I'd drunk too much champagne, didn't know where I was, and had lost my car, but I had no choice. Then I remembered that she had said something about going down to the college to print leaflets – she probably wasn't even home.

I began to feel like crying again and almost wished I had stayed put at the horrible party, waiting for Grant to collect me like a piece of luggage. Then I realized that the street looked familiar. I came to a crossroads, and there in front of me was the Heartbreak! No wonder I was so tired. I had walked all the way from Chelsea Cove over the hill and into Rockley without noticing! I almost cried with relief this time. The wonderful old Heartbreak Cafe – someone would take care of me there! They wouldn't leave me in a horrible room all alone while they went to party. I stumbled up the front steps. The sign on the front door of the cafe said "Closed", but there was still a light on and I went hopefully around to the back. I could see Joe's dark curly hair as he moved through the kitchen. I ran excitedly towards the back window and hammered on it. I saw his face, surprised and suspicious, come to the back door, peer out, and recognize me.

"Debbie!" He looked worried. "What are you doing here?" He looked around the parking lot. "Where's your car?"

"That's what I'm trying to figure out," I said, trying to sound reasonable although I couldn't make my tongue work as well as I wanted it to. "I can't find my car."

He came out of the back door and walked right up to me. "Debbie?" he asked suspiciously. "Have you been drinking?"

I giggled. "Just a little champagne," I said. "It tickled my nose, but now things have started to get weird."

He took my arm very firmly. "Come and sit down for a minute," he said, leading me inside and forcing me on to the kitchen stool. "Now, let's get this straight – where were you drinking champagne?"

"At a party," I said. "A horrible party, given by a horrible girl who hates me."

"So why did you go?"

"Grant," I said. "I had to go because of Grant."

"Where's Grant now?"

"Still at the party, having fun with the horrible girl, I guess."

Joe's face clouded with anger. "Grant let you leave a party to drive home in this state?" he demanded. YES!

"He didn't exactly let me. I ran away," I confessed. "I didn't like it."

Joe continued to look angry. "Oh, I get it – Grant got you drunk and then he tried something, right?"

I started to giggle because the whole thing was so ridiculous that I couldn't find the words to explain it to Joe.

"Not right," I said. "I kept on drinking because Grant was ignoring me. He doesn't even think of trying something with me . . . he doesn't even want me up at the lake with him." The giggle turned into a little sob and my voice choked.

Joe slipped an arm round my shoulders. "It's all right. I'll take you home. Just give me a minute to finish up here and then we'll go find your car."

He bustled around, turning off lights and locking doors, then he assisted me from my stool. "Can you walk, do you think, or do you want to stay here while I find your car?"

"I'd rather ride on your bike," I said, remembering the

warm feeling I'd had as I'd clung to Joe and we'd raced up the hill.

He shook his head. "Oh, no, I'm not going to risk having you fall off on a bend. We'll find your car. Come on." He took my hand and led me out of the back door. The night air was cold, and I shivered.

"Okay," he said. "Now, can you remember where the party was?"

"It was on the beach," I said.

"Here?" Joe peered into the darkness of Rockley Beach for signs of life.

"No, not here," I said impatiently. "A beach cottage at Chelsea Cove."

"You walked here from Chelsea Cove?" he asked.

"I didn't intend to. I just couldn't find my car. I had to park quite a way away from the party and I must have walked in the wrong direction."

"Why didn't you go in Grant's car?" he asked, setting off wearily in the direction of Chelsea.

"Grant didn't know I was coming," I said. "It was a senior party. I guess I wasn't supposed to be there, but I heard Minda say she was out to get Grant and I didn't want her to."

"And what did Grant have to say about all this?" Joe asked. "You make it sound as if you women were trading him back and forth like a used car."

"Grant . . .," I began slowly, feeling like I was about to cry again, "Grant doesn't care about me at all."

"And you?" Joe asked. "Do you care about him?"

"I hate him," I said. "I hope a great big wave comes up the

beach and sweeps him and that horrible Minda out to sea and they wind up in Japan!"

We walked on. My legs were beginning to feel like jelly. When I saw a convenient wall, I sank on to it. "I'm tired," I said. "I don't want to walk any more."

"I'm not exactly crazy about walking myself," Joe said, "especially considering I've been running around at the cafe since four this afternoon, but we have to find your car or we can't get you home."

"You could let me sleep at the cafe."

"Of course I couldn't," he said. "I couldn't leave you at the cafe all night. You'd do something stupid like turn the gas on or fall down the steps."

"You could stay with me."

"Come on, get moving. We are not spending the night at the cafe!"

"Then take me home with you," I suggested. "I don't like my house anyway. It's all cold and empty and nobody ever makes me hot chocolate any more."

He took my arm and dragged me up from the wall. "When we get you home, I'll make you hot chocolate, all right?"

"Okay," I said. "Only I'm so tired. Carry me."

"Are you crazy? I can barely carry myself. Come on, you're tough. You can do it."

He slipped an arm round my waist. I could feel him supporting me.

"When I was a little girl and we went out at night, I'd always fall asleep in the car coming home," I said, "and then my dad would try to carry me up to bed without waking me.

But I'd always wake up enough to see the wall swinging past as we went bump, bump, bump up the stairs to my room. I used to feel so safe in my dad's arms."

"Unfortunately we all have to grow up," Joe said. "And we all have to find that there's no one around to carry us any more."

"You're so right," I said. "You are so, so right. We're all alone, with no one to carry us. Poor Joe . . . poor Debbie."

Joe laughed. "Come on, you maniac," he said. "You'll have me crying, too. Think of something cheerful."

"I know," I said. "Let's sing."

"Sing?"

"Yeah, when we hiked at Brownie camp, we always sang and it made the walk go faster."

"I never went to Brownie camp!" Joe said.

"But you know the songs," I insisted. "How about 'Row, Row, Row Your Boat'?"

"I'm not walking down a public street singing 'Row, Row, Row Your Boat'!" Joe said.

"Oh, come on. Sing, Joe – or you'll have to carry me. Come on: 'Row, row, row your boat, gently down the stream . . .' " I began in a slightly uncertain voice. Joe joined in, even more uncertainly. We began to walk in step, then to march, laughing as we sang. We even tried it as a round, but we both got lost and had to stop.

"You know, Grant would never do this," I commented, breathing heavily after our brisk walk. "He hates doing anything that isn't exactly correct. He even dressed as a prince for Halloween – in a rented costume. And he rented a matching princess costume for me. I'd already made myself this terrific lady vampire costume, but he insisted on the princess."

We walked on. "You know, Grant is definitely boring," I said. "He was even embarrassed when I got drunk tonight – even though he always thinks it's funny when his friends get drunk and throw each other in someone's swimming pool. I think he was embarrassed because I took a swing at Minda."

"You punched the hostess?"

"I would have flattened her, too, but Grant grabbed my arms. I told her that I'd developed great muscles from waiting tables."

I could tell Joe was chuckling beside me. "Come on, Rocky," he said. "Now I know I'd better get you home quick before you deck a cop."

The street began to look familiar. "There's the pine tree, I think."

"What pine tree?"

"The one I parked my car under," I said excitedly. "Yeah, look – there's my car!"

"Then you must have walked right past it on the way to Rockley," Joe said.

"No, I didn't, because I cut up one street behind this," I said. "I only turned on to this street down there."

"Ah," Joe said. "Well, we've found the car, thank heavens. Now the next big question is, have you got the keys?"

I patted my purse, which hung from my shoulder. "In here," I said. "I did remember to bring my purse with me."

Joe helped me into the car and started it. "Nice little car," he said. "Handles real well." He put his foot down and we sped through the night. I tried closing my eyes, but the world started swinging again, so I sat up, feeling the wind in my hair, trying to focus on the blur of houses and gardens as they flashed past us.

"Give me your address again," Joe said.

"It's up this way – an ugly condo. You can't miss it," I said. "And it has ugly rocks outside it and ugly junipers."

"What's it called?" Joe said. "I've never been to your house, remember."

"That's funny," I said, chuckling as if I'd just discovered the world's greatest joke.

"What's funny?"

"That you've never even been to my house. I feel like I've known you forever and you've never even seen the ugly rocks and the ugly junipers."

"Its name, Debbie," Joe said firmly.

"The Oaks," I said, " 'a planned community for today's family'. Planned to be horrible, that is."

"I've seen much worse than The Oaks," Joe said. "You should see where some people have to live."

"Don't you start lecturing me now," I said, "because my tongue won't work to argue with you so it's not fair."

He laughed. "Okay, fair enough."

It seemed like no time at all before we were home.

Joe got out and helped me to my front door. "Maybe it's better if I don't come in," he said on the doorstep. "I mean, your mom might not understand. She might think it was me who got you drunk."

"You wouldn't do a thing like that to a girl," I said. "You're not a lowly little worm like Grant Buckley. I'll tell my mom that you're all right, don't worry."

We opened the front door and went in. "It's okay," I said. "She's not home yet."

"Are you sure?" he asked. "Perhaps she's gone to bed."

"No. See, her purse isn't where she always puts it on the counter. A creature of habit is my mother. And she hasn't put out the cereal bowls for breakfast. She is definitely not home."

"But it's almost midnight," Joe said as if a mother not being home at this time was shocking.

"She's printing leaflets to save the salt marsh mouse," I said. "Very important stuff, saving the shalt moose mash . . . I mean the salsh mouch mowch . . . why won't my tongue do what I want it to?"

Joe laughed. "I think I'd better make you that hot chocolate like I said. Where do you keep it?"

"Above the blender," I said, tottering to stand behind him. "And the mugs are hanging up on the mug tree."

"Mug tree," he said with amusement. "That's a new concept. You go sit down and I'll make it."

"I am *so* tired," I said. "So very tired."

"Well, you can go straight to bed and sleep it off now," Joe said.

I sank on to the kitchen stool. "You make hot chocolate so well," I commented.

"It's an art," he said, laughing. "All a question of how you flick the spoon and stir in the boiling water. Here, it's ready. Don't spill it."

"It's too hot to drink," I said. "I think I'll put it on my bedside table." I started to carry it back into the bedroom.

"Give it to me," Joe said impatiently. "You're spilling it on the floor."

He carried it for me and turned on the bedside lamp. It threw a nice pink glow across the room. I sank on to the bed.

"Right, now you're all settled, okay?" Joe asked in a not-too-steady voice.

"I guess so," I said. He looked down at me uncertainly. His dark brown eyes seemed so warm, so caring. I reached out my hand and took his. "Don't go," I said. "I don't want to be left alone."

He laughed, uneasily. "What would your mother say if she came home right now?"

"She doesn't care about me," I said. "She only cares about saving her shalt mice. You're the only person in the world who cares about me. And you know what – you're much nicer than Grant. You've got the best soft brown eyes and your eyelashes curl so nicely and you know what? You kiss better than Grant, too. Kiss me, Joe."

He sank to the bed beside me. "I really ought to be going," he whispered. He took my chin into his hand and very gently brushed my lips. "There," he said. "Now go to sleep, okay?"

"No, kiss me the right way," I insisted. I wrapped my arms round his neck and pulled him towards me. "Kiss me like you did that night on the beach. You know how to kiss a girl … not like stuffy old Grant. I bet he wouldn't even know what to do if he had a girl alone in her bedroom and she wanted him to kiss her." I was gazing up at him. I saw his eyes flicker for a second as he took the back of my neck into his hand and brought his lips towards mine. I was tingling, I was floating. I was feeling the way I had never felt before. I didn't want it to ever end . . .

Chapter Sixteen

When I opened my eyes the next morning, harsh sunlight was flooding in through the gap in the drapes. I woke up slowly, like a diver coming up from deep water. Why did my head hurt so much? Was I sick? Why did it feel as if somebody were sticking needles into my eyes every time I tried to move them? Pieces of the night before began to fall into place like a jigsaw puzzle. Something about looking for a car and Grant and Minda and Joe! Suddenly I was very wide awake. Very cautiously, because the sunlight hurt my eyes, I looked round me. I was alone, in my own bed, dressed in my own clothes from the night before. I hadn't dreamed last night, had I? The last thing I remembered was begging Joe to kiss me. My face flooded with embarrassment as I tried to recall details. I could remember enough of the way I'd behaved, of what I'd said to him, to feel very uncomfortable. How could I ever face him again? And yet, I thought I remembered him not going away but instead putting his arms round me, holding me very tight, and kissing me just the way I'd always wanted to be kissed . . .

I sat up, although my head did not enjoy being moved from the pillow. The sunlight was painting a bright stripe across my carpet. I stared at it suspiciously. The sun did not reach that room until midmorning. I must have overslept. What day was it anyway? I turned to focus on the clock radio. Ten o'clock and it was Friday morning! I was way late for school. I leaped out of bed, felt horribly sick, and had to sink down on to the bed again.

So I won't go to school today, I decided. *I have been a model student for all these years, dragged myself to school with colds and sprained ankles and sore throats. Today I'll stay home and be sick.*

Even as I decided this, I felt much better. It was Friday. I wouldn't have to face Grant or Minda or anybody else until Monday, and by then they'd all be caught up in rehearsals for graduation and signing yearbooks. I pulled on my nightgown and wandered into the kitchen to put on some coffee. The rich warm smell made my appetite return and also reminded me that I had eaten almost nothing the night before. I was about to go get some cereal when I noticed my mother's purse propped on the kitchen counter. Did that mean she was still here? She usually left for school right after I did.

I crept cautiously to her bedroom and pushed open the door. She was lying on her back, sound asleep, looking relaxed and peaceful, just how I remembered her from my childhood. Seeing her face like this made me realize how very tired she had looked the past year – lots of new frown lines had appeared. As if she felt my presence, she stirred and opened her eyes.

"Why, Debbie, what's wrong?" she asked. Then she added suspiciously, "What time is it? Why aren't you at school?"

"I was going to ask you the same thing," I said quickly. "It's past ten o'clock."

"I didn't set my alarm because I got in so late last night," she said. "The stupid copying machine kept breaking down and none of us knew how to fix it and we were there until two thirty. Since I've got to go visit a marsh this afternoon, I thought I'd be very bad and skip classes."

I was still remembering the night before. She couldn't have seen Joe, or she would surely have already said something. Besides, I could hardly ask her if I was alone when she came home! "Er, Mom, you said you came home at two thirty," I said. "I guess I was sound asleep, right?"

"I guess so," she said, surprised.

"You, er, didn't check on me then?"

She looked even more surprised. "Your door was closed, your car was in your space – why should I have checked on you?"

"Uh, no reason, no reason at all. Except that you used to come and tuck me in when I was little."

She laughed and started to get out of bed. "Is that coffee I smell?" she asked.

"Um-hmm. It's almost ready," I said.

"Wonderful," she said, finding her slippers and standing up. "I'm glad you stayed – *why did* you stay home? Are you sick? You don't look too well."

"That's it," I said. "I'm sick. I've got a terrible headache. And my stomach, too."

"Summer flu. There's a lot of it going round the college," my mother said. "You poor thing. Get back to bed. Do you want to try and eat anything?"

"An egg," I said hesitantly, because I was feeling a little

guilty about claiming to be sick. "I'd love a boiled egg, like you used to make me when I was little when I was sick."

She laughed. "With lots of bread and butter fingers around it to dip in the yolk?"

"That's right," I said.

She started for the kitchen. "You are funny," she said. "Most of the time I think of you as a young woman, but there are times when I remember that you're really still a little girl in ways."

"I think I liked being a little girl much better," I said. "It was less complicated."

She smiled. "You wait. You'll find there are some good things about being grown up, too. Go on, get back to bed with you."

I obeyed, enjoying the coolness of the sheets, the softness of my pillow. I sat up to eat my egg from a tray, dipping in the fingers of bread and eating all the yolk first, just the way I used to. When I had finished, I even turned the shell upside down. I always used to do that and then I'd give the egg to my father, who would pretend to crack it and find nothing inside. I stopped, conscious of the ache of emptiness. My father would never be there again to crack eggs. The old days had gone and nothing could bring them back again. However hard I tried, I could not go back to being a little girl again.

I lay back and waited for my mother to take the tray. She came in, dressed in jeans and a sweatshirt. "Sorry, I have to run now," she said, "but we're meeting to drive to the marsh at noon."

"Ah yes, the shalt moosh mace," I said, giggling.

"The what?"

"Nothing," I said. "Have a good time."

She stood looking down at me. "I don't like to leave you when you're not feeling well," she said. "Are you sure you'll be all right?"

"I'm sure," I said. "I'll have to be up for work at four anyway."

"Oh, honey, you can't go in to work," my mother said in a firm mother voice. "Phone them and tell them you're sick."

"There's only Joe," I said, feeling the colour rush to my cheeks when I mentioned his name. "He could never handle Fridays alone."

My mother noticed the blush. "I hope you're not running a fever," she said."Maybe I should take you in to Dr O'Brien?"

"I'll be fine. You'd better go. Your friends are waiting for you."

She looked worried, torn between her duty to me and the waiting salt marsh mouse. "Debbie, I don't know," she said. "I really don't want you going to work. All that running around in a hot kitchen . . ."

"I'll be fine," I said. "I bet it's just a twenty-four-hour bug. I'll be over it by afternoon."

"That would be an eight-hour variety," she said, with a little chuckle, "but I guess you know how you feel and you're old enough to make your own decisions. Just promise me you'll stay in bed until then. I don't want to be worrying about you overdoing it when I should be tramping through marshes."

"Okay. I'll stay in bed," I said. "Right now I have no great desire to get up. I think I'll go back to sleep again."

"Good idea," she said. She turned to go, then hesitated at the door. "Well, see you tonight, then," she said. "Late again, I imagine. It's quite a drive to the salt marsh."

By lunchtime I was feeling surprisingly well. I sat on the sofa and watched reruns on TV, enjoying the feeling of being the only person not working in the entire world. Then, around four, I drove to the cafe. I had considered chickening out hundreds of times, planning all the things I would say when I called Joe, but in the end I forced myself out of the house. I had to know about the previous night, and I had to face Joe again eventually.

Joe looked up as I came into the kitchen. He eyed me appraisingly, then grinned. "You look a lot better than I expected you to," he commented. "No hangover?"

"It's gone," I said, cautiously removing my jacket and hanging it up.

"See, I knew you were tough," he said, still grinning. "And did Grant want to know where you'd disappeared to?"

"I haven't seen Grant," I said, not daring to meet his eyes. "I didn't go to school today."

"You cut classes?" Joe demanded. "Once you start on the road to ruin there's no stopping you, is there?"

"Shut up," I said, and pretended to get busy with the ketchup bottles.

After a while I couldn't stand it. "Joe?" I asked. "What exactly happened last night?"

"What do you mean, 'last night'?"

"You know very well what I mean. After you

brought me home."

"You don't remember?" He sounded hurt.

"Not exactly. I remember, er, parts."

"The best night of your life and you don't remember it?" He sounded so offended that it made me look up. His dark eyes were laughing at me, teasing and amused. Unable to face those mocking eyes a moment longer, I grabbed the condiment tray and hurried through to the cafe with it, banging down bottles noisily on to tables. I jumped a mile when I turned to find Joe right behind me.

"Debbie?" he said, trying not to smile. "Debbie, you didn't really think that you and I . . . last night, did you?"

"Of course not. Of course I didn't," I said hurriedly, forcing a laugh that must have sounded very fake.

A grin was spreading across his face. "You did think it! Boy, that's funny. I bet you worried all morning."

"Shut up, Joe," I said, and tried to turn away. He came up behind me again. "Debbie," he said again, "nothing happened last night. You did a lot of talking, I remember, about how much nicer I was than Grant, and how much sexier. And then you kept begging me to kiss you and you dragged me on to your bed, and then" – long pause – "and then you fell asleep. And I went home."

"Oh," I said, feeling relieved and disappointed at the same time. "How did you get home?" It was a good four miles down to the cafe from our house.

"I called a cab," he said. "I thought I'd done enough hiking for one night – or don't you remember that part either?"

"Oh yes," I said. "I remember that part." I played nervously with the tray in my hands. "Joe . . . I'm sorry. Thanks for taking care of me."

"It's all right," he said.

"No, I mean it. It was very sweet of you to help me find my car and then to drive me home and . . . and put me to bed. I'm sure I was acting very dumb – and not at all like me."

"It was a hard job," he said seriously, "but someone had to do it!" Then he started to chuckle as he walked ahead of me back to the kitchen.

After that we were pretty busy. Customers started arriving, orders came in like crazy, and we didn't have time to think of anything except who got the extra cheese and who got the fries. Then, around six thirty, I came running out with four orders balanced on my arms and almost bumped into Grant.

"Oh, Debbie," he said uneasily.

"What are you doing here?" I demanded.

"I came to see you."

"Let me give these customers their food first," I said, and pushed past him to the table in the corner.

"I just wanted to make sure you were okay," he said, walking behind me into the kitchen.

"I'm fine," I said evenly. "You took your time to find out, didn't you?"

"I drove past your place last night," he said. "I saw your car was where it should be so I figured you'd found your way home safely."

"No thanks to you," I said angrily. "For all you cared, I could have been wrapped around a lamppost by now."

"I told you to stay put and I'd drive you home later," he

said huffily.

"You treated me like a piece of baggage," I said, "while you and Minda went off together."

"I hate to remind you, but you were in no state to do anything," Grant said. "You were bombed out of your skull." He paused. "You were very foolish to try and drive home," he went on. "I was worried when we came in and saw you had gone. I'm surprised you managed to make it on your own."

"She wasn't on her own," Joe said, looking up from the grill where he had been watching burgers with his back to us as if he were part of the scenery. "She spent the night with me."

Grant's face flushed a rich tomato colour. "She did what?"

"You heard," Joe said. He looked super-cool, all his former arrogance directed at Grant. "I found her wandering around and I rescued her," he said. "Then I took her home. She didn't want to be left alone, so I stayed." He put so much meaning into that last phrase that Grant looked at me accusingly.

"Is this true, Debbie?"

I had a horrible desire to giggle, but I forced my lips not to twitch as I said, "Yes, Grant, it's true."

Grant looked from Joe to me. "She was drunk," he said angrily. "She didn't know what she was doing."

"She had a pretty good idea," Joe said. "Oh, and she also said that she thought I was sexier than you."

I'd thought Grant's face was red before. Now it positively turned purple. "I never thought you'd sink to this, Debbie," he said. "First the condo, then the cafe ... but not ... *him!*"

The giggle threatened to burst through at any moment.

"Maybe I don't belong with your group any more, Grant,"

I said. "Maybe you'd be happier with Minda."

"Maybe I would," he said. "I'm sorry to see us part like this, Debbie, but after last night, I'm afraid—"

"It's all right, Grant," I said. "I'll survive without you. Like Joe said, I'm tough. I never knew it before, but I really am tough."

Grant half turned towards the door. "I'd better be going," he said. "Goodbye, Debbie."

"Goodbye, Grant, enjoy Harvard and the lake and Minda . . ."

For a moment I thought he was going to shake my hand. He held his hand out, thought better of it, and dropped it again. Then he turned abruptly and began to walk out of the kitchen.

"Oh, and one more thing," Joe called after him. "You can't use her jokes in your speech. Try it and she'll leap up and yell that you stole them!" omg YESS!

Grant shot a worried look back through the kitchen door and then left. Joe and I looked at each other and burst out laughing.

"I'm sorry, Debbie," Joe managed to say at last, "but he had it coming to him. His face when I told him we spent the night together . . ." and he started to laugh again, holding on to the edge of the sink because he was shaking so hard. "You're not mad at me, are you?"

"Why should I be mad?" I asked.

"Because I helped you break up with your boyfriend. You may never find anyone so perfect again."

"Or so boring and conceited and selfish," I commented.

"I could easily have denied everything you told him, Joe. Actually, I enjoyed watching his face, too. He let me down pretty badly last night. He deserved everything he got."

"Do you think he'll go straight home and rewrite his speech?" Joe asked.

"He'll be out of luck if he wants Minda to help him with it," I said. "The only thing she ever reads is the flyers from the mall."

"Can we have some service out here? We've been waiting for hours!" a loud voice shouted through the kitchen door. Joe and I looked at each other and grinned. I picked up my pad.

"You said you owed me a favour," I said as I began to walk into the cafe. "I guess now we're even again."

is it really a favor if hes being waiting months to do it though??

Chapter Seventeen

On my way home that evening I did some serious thinking. Major changes had happened in my life, and yet I didn't feel all that upset. I had officially broken up with Grant and I felt more relieved than anything. I even sang as I drove up the canyon, as if a big load had been lifted from my shoulders. "No more pretending!" I said to myself, and then instantly wondered why I had said it. Had I been pretending when I was with Grant? I'd genuinely been happy with him, hadn't I – until near the end, anyhow; until I'd started working at the Heartbreak and met Joe and had my ideas on life shaken up. I tried to decide when I'd begun to feel discontented with Grant. Was it after I started working that I realized I didn't belong with him, that his world, his lack of humour, his constant striving for success bored me? I found I couldn't put a date on it, but it was clear to me that I had gone on dating him much longer than I should have.

Joe was right, I admitted to myself. I had kept hanging around with Grant because I liked how important it made me. I loved being prom queen and having my picture taken. I loved going to those awards banquets and seeing the faces looking at me in admiration when I walked through the halls at school.

I shifted uneasily as I pulled to a stop at a light. I was only just now beginning to realize that I was as bad as the rest of them. I had been mad at Joe and Grant and the other kids, too, for being attracted by a phony movie world and for trying to be something they were not. I had been extra mad at Joe because I thought he was like me – above all that sort of stuff. Now I saw that I was just like the rest of them. I had let an image be more important than my real self. Even though nobody was in the car with me, I blushed guiltily.

From now on, I promised myself, *I'm not going to be influenced by what other people say or think about me. I'm going to be me and not try to fit in with what's popular or fashionable or any of the other restrictions the kids at school put on their lives. I'm free of Grant. I won't have to hang around with Minda or anybody like her ever again. And I've got Joe to thank. Strange that I should be in his debt. I'll never let him know how much!*

I grinned to myself as the light changed and I shot away with a loud roar of engine.

When I opened the front door the first thing I saw was my mother. She was sprawled in the middle of the sofa, wearing just her bathrobe, her feet dangling into a bowl of water. Her eyes were closed and her face was ashen.

"Mom?" I whispered, sitting down gently beside her.

"Don't ask," she muttered, still not opening her eyes.

"What's wrong?" I asked anyway. "Have you got that flu you said was going around?"

"Most probably," she groaned, "along with pneumonia, and a few other things."

"Can I get you something? Some hot tea maybe?"

"That would be nice, thank you," she muttered. "I think I'm maybe strong enough to lift a cup to my lips now."

I crept through to the kitchen and filled the kettle. "Do you think I should drive you to a doctor?" I asked worriedly.

She gave a tired smile. "I don't need a doctor. I'm just suffering from plain old exhaustion."

"Oh," I said, beginning to understand. "The salt marsh mouse?"

"Don't ever mention that creature's name to me again," she said, sitting up with a groan.

"Did it attack you?" I asked, and tried not to giggle. She looked so wiped out and yet the whole thing was funny in a way.

She scowled. "There was not one amusing thing that happened all day as far as I'm concerned," she said. "In fact, that whole day was one long, horrible nightmare. To begin with, they crammed six people into my car. I had to drive with this fat shoulder in my face down all these twisting little roads – and what's more, the guy smelled as if he hadn't had a bath in a week. Then we finally got to the salt marsh."

She paused as I walked across to the boiling kettle. "Go on," I said, "this is exciting."

"Thrilling," she said with another scowl. "We finally got to the salt marsh and they gave us these big wading boots because we had to walk through marsh. Mine were about ten sizes too large and so heavy I could hardly lift one foot at a time. Well, after about a hundred yards I got my first blister and I was drenched with sweat. It was all thick mud and you had to pull each foot out with a horrible sucking sound before you could walk on. I began to think that if I stayed where I was, I'd just sink into the mud."

I came back to her with the tea. She took it and sniffed appreciatively.

"What exactly were you supposed to be doing?" I asked. "Was this a protest?"

"A survey," she said. "We were supposed to survey to find out approximately how many mice there were in one area of marsh."

"How do you do that?"

"You look out for mouse droppings," she said bitterly.

"Mouse droppings?" I suited to giggle. "You're joking, right?"

She shook her head sadly. "Deadly serious," she said. "We were told to look for signs of active habitation. Among those were nests, footprints, and droppings. Have you ever tried finding a mouse dropping in a marsh?"

I was still giggling. "I can't believe you tramped over a marsh looking for mouse droppings!"

"Did I mention that it had begun to rain by this time?" she asked. "No? Well, it had begun to rain – that sort of fine misty rain that soaks through everything. It made the bog twice as boggy, too. I began to get very tired and then my boot came off. Nobody came back to help me – they just yelled that I should hurry up. So I tried to hurry and I fell flat on my face in the mud."

"Oh, no," I said, looking at her with sympathy and trying not to smile at the same time. "You poor thing."

"That mud stinks," she said. "And you know what? They

all laughed. Nobody came to help me! They just stood there laughing, except for one little creep who told me that I'd just wrecked the ecosystem of the marsh habitat."

"So did you go home then?" I asked.

"No way! I wanted to go back to the car but nobody would hear of it. I had this horrible desire to creep back and drive home and leave them stranded—"

"You should have!" I interrupted. "Those guys were supposed to be your friends!"

"Some friends," she said. "I discovered something today! They don't give a damn about people, just stupid mice and snails and bald eagles. People can go to hell as far as they care."

I slipped my arm round her shoulder. "Well, at least you discovered it before they made you lie down in front of a bulldozer," I said.

She nodded and smiled. "You know what I kept thinking all day," she asked, "as I plodded through the horrible mud? I kept thinking about you and how I'd left my sick daughter behind for the sake of a stupid mouse. I even began to imagine that falling down in the mud was a punishment for failing as a mother!"

"Oh, come on, Mom," I said. "I wasn't that sick anyway and I am big enough to take care of myself."

"But I have been neglecting you lately, haven't I?" she asked. "I've been so wound up in this conservation stuff that I've hardly spoken a word to you in weeks."

"It's fine, really," I assured her. "You have to do your own thing, as they say."

She took a sip of the tea. "I don't think it was my own thing," she said softly. "I think you were right from the beginning. I don't think I really did care much about saving whales and trees and mice. Oh, don't get me wrong, I'd like them to be saved—"

"But not by you," I finished for her.

She laughed, the first time I heard her laugh in weeks. "At least not that way," she said. "I hate getting cold and wet and I feel stupid waving banners at people." She took another sip of tea and stared out over the steam. "I guess I joined the group because it gave me a feeling of belonging somewhere."

I nodded that I understood. "After your father left," she said softly, "I needed some sort of base. I suppose I was willing to take any lifeline that was thrown to me. Those kids seemed so friendly to begin with. They really made me feel that I—" She stopped, swallowing hard to stop her voice from breaking.

"They were just using you," I said angrily. "I could tell that all along. You had the car and the food and the place to hang out."

"You're right," she said. "I see that now. I was just so anxious to fit in, to have a place."

"I do understand, Mom," I said. "I know just how you were feeling. I've been feeling the same way myself. I don't fit in with our old crowd at the country club any more, and I'm not really one of the crowd at the cafe. It's like I'm torn between two worlds and I'm on the outside of both of them. It hurts sometimes."

"At least you have Grant," she said, "and Pam at school."

"Pam," I said. "Strike Grant."

"You and Grant have split up? When?"

"Last night," I said, "Or rather, last night made it more final. It was the same problem, Mom. We live in different worlds now. We don't even speak the same language any more. I think Joe was right. He said I only stuck around for the awards banquets and I think in a way I did."

"Joe?" she asked. "He's the young man at the cafe? The one with the hair and the bad manners?"

"That's the one," I said, grinning.

"And you like him now?"

"Sometimes," I said.

"Sometimes?"

"Sometimes I want to hit him over the head with the nearest pot," I added.

"So he's not about to replace Grant?" she asked cautiously.

"I can't see that happening," I said. "For one thing, he already has a girlfriend. And for another, I think we'd kill each other within a week if we ever got together. Anyway, he doesn't think of me that way at all. I'm just a person for him to tease most of the time."

"I see," my mother said. "Well, that's good. Maybe you and I can have some peace round here for a while. We deserve it, don't you think?"

"Maybe," I said. "I could do with a rest."

"Maybe we can go somewhere this summer," she went on. "Nowhere expensive, but we still have friends with summer cottages – just get away for a couple of weeks."

"I'd like that," I said.

"The lake, maybe?" my mother asked.

"Anywhere but the lake," I said quickly. "How about the salt marsh?"

She shuddered. "Anywhere but the salt marsh," she said.

"Did you ever see this famous salt marsh mouse?"

"Yes," she said with a shudder. "They caught one. It was just a plain little brown mouse. It looked exactly like the disgusting little vermin you put traps down for in the house!"

I started to laugh and she joined in. "Oh, Debbie," she said, "if you could have seen me: boots up to my thighs, slithering round in that mud, and at the end of it they hold up this horrid little brown mouse and everyone says, 'Oh, how darling, how cute,' and all I'm thinking is, where's the rat poison!"

"Look on it as a growth experience," I said, "and Mom – next time you decide to join a group, join one whose members are on a permanent fast. We haven't had any food in the house for weeks!"

"No more groups," my mother said. "I hope I'll start making friends, real friends, eventually, but until then I'll make do with a daughter."

We smiled at each other. "I know, let's go shopping this weekend," I said. "We haven't been since … since we moved here."

"On one condition," my mother said.

"That we don't spend much?"

"That you push me round in a shopping cart," my mother said. "My feet are killing me!"

Chapter Eighteen

On Sunday the movie crew threw a big beach party for the citizens of Rockley Beach to thank them for tolerating all the filming chaos of the past few weeks. In the late afternoon Joe's grandfather, Mr Garbarini, came down to the cafe, "to get the old horse back in the harness again", as he put it. He looked a little pale, a little more hollowed round the cheeks and eyes, his eyebrows even more like two bushy prawns than usual, but otherwise pretty healthy.

"Where is everybody?" he boomed, looking round the empty restaurant. "A month away from my cafe and you drive away all my customers!"

"There's a beach party with free food," I said. "That's where everybody is today. The movie company is hosting it."

Mr Garbarini sniffed. "Movie company! I already heard too much about this stupido movie company! I got no time for people who make these dumb pictures – spaceships and monsters and all that nonsense. And I got even less time for people who pay money to go see it!"

"I see the long rest hasn't improved his temper," Joe muttered as he passed me.

"I heard that," his grandfather bellowed. "There's nothing wrong with my hearing, thank the good Lord. Now why don't you both clear out of here and give me some peace. Take this young lady down to the beach party, you hear me! She deserves a break after all that extra work you made her do!"

"Extra work *she* had to do?" Joe shouted. "I like that. Who was here every day? Who didn't get a single weekend off to go places with his senior class? Huh? You tell me that!"

I looked across at Joe. "It's all right," I said. "I'm sure you'd rather not go down to the beach."

"Might as well," he said. "First time off I've been given in a month! When I think of all the overtime *he* owes me . . ." He turned to glare at his grandfather, who glared back. It looked like things were back to normal around the Heartbreak Cafe. Joe nodded to me. "Come on," he said. "Let's go and eat their free food."

We wandered down on to the beach. Rockley Beach was normally pretty crowded in summer. Now it was jam-packed. We grabbed ourselves hot dogs and drinks and forced our way through the crowd to the water's edge.

"I don't think I want to stay here too long," Joe said. "I don't go for crowds too much."

"Me neither," I said.

Ashley came running up to us excitedly waving a piece of paper. "I finally did it!" she shrieked. "I finally really did it!"

"A Hollywood contract?" Joe asked.

"Troy Heller's autograph!" she shrieked excitedly. "He gave it to me and said, 'Here, sweetie'!" She gave a big sigh. "I can't believe it. It's a miracle!"

And she wandered off again, a heavenly smile on her

face. Joe's eyes caught mine. "They say little things please little minds," he said. "It sure didn't take much to make her happy."

"I could get you Troy Heller's autograph, too, if you'd like," I said sweetly.

"And I could pick you up and dump you in the ocean," he said.

"You wouldn't dare!"

"Wouldn't I?" He began to sweep me up into his arms.

"Joe, put me down," I shrieked. He laughed and lowered me to the sand. "I still can't understand this Troy Heller business," he said thoughtfully. "I mean, the guy's not even great-looking, like me."

"I can see you're back to being your old self," I commented. "Modest, humble . . ."

He ignored me. "Maybe if I practised saying, 'here, sweetie'," he went on. He tried it a couple of times. I began to giggle.

"It's not fair what that guy has done for my ego," he said. "Just once I'd have loved to get the better of him – to see him look a fool."

"That's not nice, and besides, it won't happen," I said. "So eat your hot dog and stop brooding. The movie will be great for business, just like you said."

"And we'll be working our tails off," he said. "I've got to talk to Poppa about hiring another person to wait tables."

"You want to replace me?"

"Don't you dare quit!" he said. "We might get someone who was quick and efficient and knew how to do her job – then I'd have no one to yell at! Besides, who would I fight with? I just want us both to get a little free time."

"It would be nice," I said. "Imagine a whole weekend off . . ."

"A cabin at the lake?" he teased.

"Don't you start," I said.

Suddenly there was a great commotion beside the ocean. "Shark, shark!" people were screaming. It was just like the movie – everyone running up the beach in a panic, screaming and fighting to get away from the edge of the ocean. Joe grabbed me and held me firmly as the crowd swept past us. Troy Heller ran by, his mouth open in panic. "Shark, shark!" he was screaming like everyone else. As he drew even with us he stumbled in the soft sand. The crowd poured over him. Flailing his way through the crowd like a salmon going upstream, Harris Barclay appeared, tripped over Troy, staggered to his feet again, and ran on shouting, "Don't panic. Everyone stay calm, just save Mr Russom!"

Joe hauled Troy to his feet. Troy wiped the sand from his face and blurted out a few words his fans probably didn't know were in his vocabulary. He described Rockley Beach in a way that would have made his publicist have an instant heart attack, then he staggered on without a word of thanks. I peered through the crowd and caught a glimpse of an enormous fin. Closer and closer to the shore it came. A great head emerged from the water, then horrible teeth . . .

"Wait a minute," Joe said. "Sharks don't breathe air!"

We ran to the water's edge, which was now deserted.

"Howard!" Joe yelled. "Are you in there?"

The head opened and Howard's excited face peeked out.

"Did I scare them? Do you think they'll give me a special effects contract?" he asked.

Joe started to laugh. "I think they've just gone for harpoon guns to destroy you," he said, "but you made Troy Heller fall flat on his face in the sand as he hurried to get away, and that was good enough for me."

"I think you were terrific," I added. "You stole the show. At least you'll get more publicity than they will today!"

Sure enough, reporters from local news stations and newspapers converged round Howard. Joe and I drifted away from the crush at the water's edge.

"He's pretty talented, actually," Joe commented. "That was a realistic-looking shark's head. I wouldn't be surprised if he didn't end up working in special effects."

"Nothing would surprise me about the people at the Heartbreak," I said. "I am now prepared for anything to happen while I'm around you guys."

He grinned. "We'll have to think of something to make you lose your cool," he said. "Maybe get you drunk again – that breaks down your frosty exterior very nicely."

"I don't want to talk about it," I said, starting to walk up the beach towards the rocks. "I still feel like a fool."

Joe came after me. He put his hand on my arm. "Debbie," he said. "I want to tell you something."

"Yes?"

He looked at me steadily. "I told you nothing happened the other night. It didn't mean that I wasn't . . . tempted. But it wouldn't have been right. Anyway, I wanted you to know that – you know what I mean?"

"It's very sweet of you to say that, Joe," I muttered.

His old, wicked, confident smile flashed across his face. "Let me tell you something," he said slowly and deliberately. "When you and I finally get together, I guarantee you that you will not forget it by the next morning!"

I watched him stroll up the beach ahead of me, walking easily over the soft sand. *There's nothing wrong with that guy's self-confidence,* I thought with a smile. *Mr Macho of Rockley Beach strikes again!* All the same, I found myself feeling strangely excited because I'd noted he had said "when" instead of "if". Could there really be a time in the future when Joe and I would get together? He must have sensed me staring at his back because he turned round.

"What do you think you've got, the whole day off?" he called back to me. "There's five pounds of onions waiting to be cut up in the kitchen, and I'm not risking letting customers see me cry. That leaves you!"

"You're all heart," I called back. "And I hope you'll let me know if you ever see any pork chops with feathers on them when you're in the butcher shop."

"Why?" he asked, puzzled.

"Because the day you and I get together will be the day that pigs fly!" I shouted. Then I ran up the beach, pushing ahead of him until it turned into a flat-out race back to the cafe.

Aww I love them

Heartbreak Café

1

NO EXPERIENCE REQUIRED

JANET QUIN-HARKIN

It's 1989. Life's easy for DEBORAH LESLEY: she's up-market, drives her own flash car to school, and looks pretty good too. She's never had a job, either; but now her parents have split up, and she needs the money.

JOE GARBARINI is cool. He likes motorbikes, girls, and fun. He doesn't have time for much — he's running Heartbreak Cafe when he's not at school.

The Heartbreak Cafe is a noisy hangout on the north Californian coast. Joe's worked there for years, and knows what it takes. He's sure Debbie won't last a month — but Debbie's determined to put up with his wisecracks and prove him wrong.

Debbie, Joe and the rest of the gang are all at the Heartbreak Cafe. Meet them in this sparkling new series from bestselling author Janet Quin-Harkin.

www.HeartbreakCafe.LA

Heartbreak Café

3

AT YOUR SERVICE

JANET QUIN-HARKIN

Nothing seems to be going right for Debbie Lesley and her first ever job at the Heartbreak Café. She and Joe Garbarini — who runs the place — don't often have a civil word for each other, and to make matters worse, Joe's glamorous girlfriend Wendy takes over Debbie's daytime shift. Then the sparks really fly, and Debbie's desperate. She doesn't know where to turn. Her best friend Pam has taken up with a drag-racing rock singer, her boyfriend Grant is now an ex-boyfriend, and even her mother is going out on dates. What's happening to her life?

Read about Debbie and Joe and the rest of the gang in this third book in the Heartbreak Café series by best-selling author Janet Quin-Harkin.

www.HeartbreakCafe.LA

Heartbreak Café

4

CATCH OF THE DAY

JANET QUIN-HARKIN

It's a busy summer at the Heartbreak Cafe, but Deborah Leslie has got more than her job as a waitress to deal with.

She still doesn't know where she stands with Joe Garbarini — they spend all their time hurling insults at each other across the kitchen — and even her father doesn't seem to need her any more. Then there's her friend Art, a typical Californian surfer, without a care in the world — until he falls for a beautiful Mexican girl he saved from drowning. Only Debbie knows the danger Art is in, but to help him she's going to need Joe's support.

The rest of the gang are also here with Debbie and Joe in this fourth book in the Heartbreak Cafe series by best-selling author Janet Quin-Harkin.

www.HeartbreakCafe.LA

Heartbreak Café

5

LOVE TO GO

JANET QUIN-HARKIN

At last everything is going right for Deborah Lesley— her best friend is working with her at the Heartbreak Cafe, it's a beautiful summer, and now Joe Garbarini, the cool, macho manager, has finally decided that they make a great couple . . .

But Debbie feels instinctively that trouble is on the way when a mysterious girl, dressed in black, appears in the cafe. Maybe she's being paranoid — Joe thinks she's over-reacting again — but Debbie is determined to stick to her principles.

The rest of the gang are all here in this fifth book in the Heartbreak Cafe series by bestselling author Janet Quin-Harkin.

www.HeartbreakCafe.LA

Heartbreak Café

6

JUST DESSERTS

JANET QUIN-HARKIN

Deborah Lesley and Joe Garbarini appear at last to have settled into a stable relationship, and with everything going smoothly at the Heartbreak Cafe, life seems pretty good.

Then a big development corporation descends on Rockley Beach and the calm is shattered.

Will Joe and his grandfather sell the Heartbreak. Debbie finds herself caught in the middle and once again her life is in turmoil . . .

The rest of the gang are all here again with Debbie and Joe in this sixth book in the Heartbreak Cafe series by bestselling author Janet Quin-Harkin.

Publisher - Feb 2021

Printed in Great Britain
by Amazon

57722515R00125